BLUE HEAVEN

The OFFICIAL Chelsea books:

Chelsea's Cup Glories by Paul Roberts

Football Fitness by Ade Mafe

Chelsea! The Ultimate Fan Book by Pete Collins

The Official Chelsea Fact File by Neil Barnett

The Bridge: Behind the Scenes at Chelsea by John Nicholson and Oliver Holt

The Chelsea Who's Who by Rick Glanvill

The Official Chelsea Quiz Book by Neil Barnett

The Official Chelsea Quote Book by Neil Barnett

Chelsea is Our Name:
A Collection of Fans' Tributes, Memories and Stories of Chelsea Football Club

BLUE HEAVEN

The Full Story of Chelsea's Historic 1997/98 Season

Neil Barnett

B🌼XTREE

MACMILLAN

First published in 1998 by Boxtree, an imprint of Macmillan Publishers Ltd,
25 Eccleston Place, London, SW1W 9NF and Basingstoke

Associated companies throughout the world

ISBN 0 7522 2483 2

All photographs courtesy Action Images except pages 12, 22, 26, 34, 70, 73, 80, 104, 110, 112, 114 & 125 courtesy Steev Burgess and 103, 126 (bottom) and 127 courtesy Neil Barnett

9 8 7 6 5 4 3 2 1

A CIP catalogue record for this book is available from the British Library

Designed by DW Design, London

Printed by Bath Press

Prepress origination by Speedscan Ltd

CONTENTS

Foreword by Gianluca Vialli

This is the story of one of the most successful and dramatic seasons in Chelsea's history. We have won two trophies for the first time ever. We have finished in the top four for only the fifth time in our history. And we have changed our manager from Ruud Gullit to myself.

After I signed for Chelsea as a player in May 1996, a man was brought to my hotel room in Torino and introduced to me as the 'Spy'. It was Neil Barnett, who had flown over to cover my move for Chelsea's publications and *Clubcall*.

Everyone calls him 'Spy' because he is always at training, always at games and we can't get rid of him no matter how hard we try. That is why we threw him fully clothed into the bath at Wembley after we won the Coca-Cola Cup. There is no-one better to tell the truth about what *really* happened in this extraordinary year.

Ciao.

Spy in the bath: Neil Barnett captured by Chelsea fitness and conditioning coach Ade Mafe in Wembley's dressing room after the Coca-Cola Cup Final

Introduction

I first started watching Chelsea in early 1960. The team of 1997/98 is without doubt the best that I have seen. The football of the first few months was unique and the trophies won in the last two months were richly deserved.

The togetherness of the players was also better than at any time since I started working with the club in 1986. The mixture of veterans, long-stayers, overseas stars and brash young hopefuls became a remarkably happy blend.

But football clubs aren't easy places. They are full of climaxes and troughs, happy players in the team and frustrated players out of it, desperate players with injuries, worried players approaching the end of their contracts, cock-a-hoop players in form and introverted players out of form.

Chelsea is never an easy place to be. Who else would part company with their manager when second in the League!

From my privileged position, at the training ground every day and around the dressing room at games, I saw it all. This is the real Chelsea story, warts and all, in a wonderful year.

It runs game by game, but the year's story unfolds through each event. Statistics include 'assists' which are given not for the final pass but for a crucial part played in a goal. Some goals have no assists, some have more than one. 'The Team' section records each player's number of starts, substitute appearances and goals.

Chelsea is a unique football club. Its supporters have endured generations of mediocrity and several potentially outstanding teams being ruined by strange management. Suddenly, those supporters are witnessing glory. They deserve this story.

Neil Barnett
May 1998

The Season

Sunday 3 August
Wembley Stadium
73,636

Chelsea 1 Manchester United 1

CHELSEA LOST 4–2 ON PENALTIES

Sunshine, celebration, and a little bit of needle in the air. Chelsea contested the Charity Shield for the third time in our history, for the second time as FA Cup winners. We had made five summer signings, we had broken the duck of twenty-six years without silverware, and we were full of optimism.

And here to face us was Manchester United, the team which thumped us 4–0 in the 1994 FA Cup Final with the crucial aid of a controversial penalty decision. United achieved the Double that year, but Premiership runners-up Blackburn were invited to the Charity Shield rather than Chelsea. Now we were here in our own right.

And after all the pre-season preparation, unbeaten in six games, here was our first opportunity to see player-manager Ruud Gullit's top selection.

His back four had looked regular throughout pre-season. His front two had rotated, and now the premier choice of last season, Hughes and Zola, got the vote.

In midfield Wise had overcome a summer operation and was ready to start his first game. Petrescu had been suffering with a virus, and eighteen-year-old Morris, who had enjoyed a good pre-season on the back of England's Under-20 World Cup campaign, got his chance in preference to the Romanian. What a chance!

The balance Gullit chose had Morris in the anchor midfield role, and to accommodate summer signing Poyet, Di Matteo moved from the front of the midfield diamond to the left.

Wembley was almost at capacity, the joy of being there was in the air; the full chorus of songs was aired. Everyone knew that Ruud Gullit wasn't too concerned by the score. To him this was little more than a *big* pre-season friendly. But to Chelsea fans and players this was Chelsea v Manchester United. Not so much scores to settle as pride to be protected.

United started by far the stronger. Nothing pretty-pretty, they powered long balls over Chelsea's midfield for debut striker Sheringham and Cole to knock down and chase. Chelsea didn't seem to have the power to counter this.

Early on Scholes broke clear but shot too close to de Goey, who was making his debut in goal, and for Chelsea Clarke made two important interceptions.

Mark Hughes heads in the first goal of the season

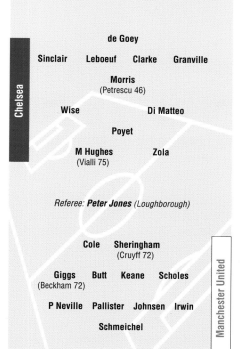

Chelsea

de Goey

Sinclair   Leboeuf   Clarke   Granville

Morris
(Petrescu 46)

Wise   Di Matteo

Poyet

M Hughes   Zola
(Vialli 75)

*Referee: **Peter Jones** (Loughborough)*

Cole   Sheringham
(Cruyff 72)

Giggs   Butt   Keane   Scholes
(Beckham 72)

P Neville Pallister Johnsen Irwin

Schmeichel

Manchester United

After a quarter of an hour Gullit switched Wise and Morris, putting the experienced captain in the anchor midfield role. Immediately Chelsea were more combative. The game became combative too.

Chelsea penetrated now with Zola only being denied by Pallister's terrific tackle as he raced onto Di Matteo's chip, and Hughes headed a Morris cross straight at Schmeichel.

United had no intention of losing to a team widely seen throughout the land as one of the few which might challenge them for the Championship. Tackles flew in – Wembley was witnessing a serious contest.

When United captain Keane dived in so recklessly on Poyet that he caught him in the head with his boot, tempers grew frayed. Keane somehow escaped the referee's book – welcome to English football, Gus – but Sinclair and Wise were booked for fouls in the next five minutes and the game threatened to get out of hand.

Five minutes before half-time Chelsea's best move so far, which started at the back with Leboeuf and finished with Zola cleverly laying the ball back from the left for Poyet, who sliced wide, suggested Chelsea were now in the driving seat.

Before the interval Sheringham was booked for elbowing Clarke amidst more angry scenes, and the same player then missed the target when well placed from Giggs' flick.

Petrescu replaced Morris at half-time and Chelsea continued to improve. Zola forced Schmeichel to scramble

away a twenty-five-yard left-footer, and then the breakthrough came on fifty-two minutes. In the end it was a surprise.

Hughes lost his marker at a corner, and as Zola's ball swung in Schmeichel stayed rooted to his line. Hughes was well inside the six-yard box as he ran on to the ball and thudded a header past the goalkeeper.

United's equalizer came four minutes later. Johnsen escaped Granville at Giggs' outswinging corner and his header found the near post unmanned. De Goey could only help the ball in. No more having a man on the back post only at corners!

Early season rustiness set in, and a draw became the obvious outcome. Butt's challenges irked, but he got away with them. Wise's challenges annoyed United manager Alex Ferguson who remarked afterwards: 'I think Dennis Wise and a football field can cause trouble.'

Sinclair's superb tackle on substitute Cruyff ensured the game went to a penalty shoot-out. No extra time this early in the season.

Gullit stood with Ferguson to watch and joked and laughed throughout. He had what he wanted, a draw with the champions – equal stature. The result of the shoot-out was secondary.

Chelsea went first, and Sinclair's drive was easily blocked by Schmeichel. Di Matteo, going third, blasted over from a short run up.

And so the Charity Shield was lost. It wasn't a great game, but pride was maintained. A bit of needle remained. Roll on the season.

> *To lose by penalties I don't mind so much because it is a lottery. I just give my judgment on what happens on the pitch. Both teams didn't play very well. From our point of view it was a festival of bad passing, bad mistakes. They were more dangerous when we had the ball. It was not a good game. But I'm not disappointed at all. It was cat and mouse. From Chelsea's point of view, that means we can cope with the best there is in England.*
>
> **Ruud Gullit**

	Chelsea	Man Utd
Shots on target	3	2
Corners	5	5
Fouls	13	11
Offsides	6	8
Bookings	3	1

Sinclair, foul (25 mins), Wise, foul (27), Petrescu, dissent (88); Sheringham on Clarke (42).

	Chelsea	Man Utd
Goals	1	1
M Hughes (52); Johnsen (56)		
Assist		
Zola		
Penalties	2	4

Sinclair (saved), Scholes, Zola, Irwin, Di Matteo (missed), Keane, Leboeuf, Butt.

Saturday 9 August
Highfield Road
22,686

Coventry City 3 Chelsea 2

FIRST OPENING DAY DEFEAT FOR FOUR YEARS

The perfect first fixture. A home game was out of the question because the Shed Umbro Stand at Stamford Bridge was still being finished and the West Stand lower tier was still being developed. Coventry was not too far away and they gave our fans a whopping 4,000 seats, including some along the side of the pitch right up to the halfway line. It was like a home game.

The same fixture last season had ended in a stupid 3–1 defeat after we had led at the interval, so there was everything to gain. And Chelsea had enjoyed the extra stimulus of making a club record signing the day before. Graeme Le Saux, a Ruud Gullit target for several months, was purchased for a Premiership record for a defender. The same Le Saux who had been sold by Chelsea to Blackburn when David Webb was manager.

But this Chelsea side boasted ten internationals, equalling the most we have ever fielded. And on the bench was Tore Andre Flo, another summer signing who originally was not expected until the end of his Brann Bergen contract in November. A cool £300,000 had secured him early.

It was another lovely day and everywhere Chelsea fans joyfully radiated optimism. Last year, at last, was our year. This one could be even better.

So what went wrong? Not a lot. Chelsea annihilated Coventry, winning the corner count 9–1, dominating possession, constantly getting into good positions and defending without problems ... or, rather, defending without problems for all but three incidents. This defeat was truly inexcusable.

Tore Andre Flo celebrates his debut goal

Managing director Colin Hutchinson said on signing him: 'It was a mistake which has taken four-and-a-half years and five million pounds to rectify.'

Early season absentees were Newton (knee operation), new signings Babayaro (groin strain and stress fracture in foot) and Lambourde (hip problem), defender Duberry (ruptured achilles since January) and goalkeeper Kharine (ruptured cruciate ligament since September 1996).

Coventry were defensive from the start. Shaw man-marked Zola, leaving the remainder of the back line to form the equivalent of a back three. So their wide midfielders were like wing-backs and marked our wide midfielders. There seemed no-one left to mark our full-backs.

Maybe it was a deliberate ploy. But somehow while Telfer and Breen sorted out the threat of Le Saux on their right, no-one bothered with Sinclair. He got so much ball and so much space.

Coventry

Ogrizovic

Breen (Boland 80)   Shaw   Williams   Burrows

Telfer   McAllister   Soltvedt   Salako

Huckerby (Lightbourne 71)   Dublin

*Referee: **Paul Durkin** (Dorset)*

Chelsea

Zola   M Hughes (Flo 67)

Di Matteo

Poyet   Petrescu

Wise

Le Saux   Clarke   Leboeuf   Sinclair

de Goey

Chelsea lorded the affair. If only the final ball into the box had been better. Good positions were constantly wasted, but Chelsea monopolized the ball and came forward again and again. Petrescu didn't shoot when he should have, Di Matteo hit over, Petrescu headed wide, long shots by Zola and Di Matteo didn't test Ogrizovic sufficiently. Eight efforts went off-target.

And then six minutes before half-time Coventry left Sinclair in space once too often. Receiving a square ball from Wise, he used a Petrescu overlap as a decoy, cut inside Salako and from just inside the area drove a left-foot shot inside Ogrizovic. Perfect timing, perfect day.

Within a minute Coventry were level with one of the most stupidly conceded goals you will ever see. Salako's long throw found Dublin unshadowed at the front – he had moved forward and then back and somehow lost Leboeuf in the process – and with de Goey remaining on his line the striker outjumped Poyet and headed directly in from eight yards.

Chelsea got rattled. Leboeuf was booked for dissent. Then, typically, he launched a forty-yard block of dynamite which nearly broke the outside of the Coventry post. Brilliant.

The second-half was the same as the first. Chelsea's balance had improved from Wembley with the simple switch of Di Matteo and Poyet. Di Matteo was far happier through the middle, and although Poyet at times was peripheral, he settled into the wide role easily enough.

Petrescu was just wide again while Poyet headed fractionally past the post. Zola and Wise were magnificent, setting up opening after opening. But with no end product, Flo replaced the quiet Hughes midway through the half. Three minutes into his debut he scored. And what a sweet goal.

He was involved in the build-up, reaching a long ball up the left. Zola and Wise switched it to Di Matteo on the right whose shot was blocked by Ogrizovic. Zola found Di Matteo again and this time he crossed. Flo ran in and thumped a header back across the goalkeeper. Oh how we all celebrated. Victory seemed inevitable. Flo was a hero.

And then in the last ten minutes Chelsea caved in twice. Coventry put on midfielder Boland for defender Breen. There seemed no threat but two goals came.

Coventry won their only corner after eighty-two minutes. McAllister curled an outswinger to the edge of the six-yard box, Dublin repeated his forward-backward movement to find freedom again, this time outjumping Flo who was behind him while de Goey again stayed on his line. All-round disaster. 2-2. And with three minutes to go Dublin claimed his hat-trick. Flo had turned villain by blasting over Petrescu's chipped cross from six yards, and now the Coventry captain was left in horrible space when Telfer's long ball sliced off Leboeuf's head, taking it away from Sinclair. Blunder after blunder. Dublin shot across de Goey without fuss. If only Chelsea had finished like that.

> *We had all the possession, all the play, played a lot of good stuff, made a lot of chances, and gave three silly goals away. If we want to win something, we'll have to defend better. When you lose goals from set pieces you haven't marked properly. The third goal should have been a consolation for them. If it's possible to put the mistakes out of your head, just think about the positive things, then it's going to be a very good season for us. But we must eliminate the silly mistakes because it's going to cost us dearly in the long run.*
>
> Steve Clarke

	Coventry	Chelsea
Shots on target	5	7
Woodwork	0	1
Corners	1	9
Fouls	15	13
Offsides	5	1
Bookings	4	3

Williams on Hughes (45), Burrows flare up with Hughes (64), Huckerby on Leboeuf (66), Lightbourne on Leboeuf (77); Wise, foul (27), Leboeuf, dissent (45), Hughes, flare up (64).

	Coventry	Chelsea
Goals	3	2

Dublin (40, 82, 87); Sinclair (39), Flo (70)

Assists
Zola, Di Matteo

Sunday 24 August
Oakwell
18,170

Barnsley 0 Chelsea 6
CHELSEA'S BIGGEST EVER AWAY WIN IN THE TOP FLIGHT

Summer drought? Yorkshire water shortage? Today brought serious rain. The car park on a field behind the ground was filled with muddy bogs, and the police horses led down from their van trod gingerly across it before reaching the terra firma of the road.

If this was to be a trophy contending year, Chelsea had something to prove. Following that first game everyone else had had a midweek fixture and then a blank weekend for internationals. Chelsea's midweek game had been scrubbed on the original fixture list so that time could be given for the Stamford Bridge developments to be finished. Defeat here could put us right at the bottom of the Premiership.

Barnsley, in the top flight for the first time, had lost their first game at home to West Ham but won their second at Crystal Palace.

Ruud Gullit put into practice his often declared intention to use the squad system to its full potential. He left out Hughes who had been involved in a rough international for Wales in Turkey, and gave Vialli his first start of the season. Vialli had been in impressive pre-season form, and with the game live on television was about to write his first of several headlines for the campaign.

Leboeuf pulled out late in the day with a stomach upset, so Myers came in to give, surely, Chelsea's shortest back four of all time: Sinclair 5ft 9in (1.75m), Clarke 5ft 10in (1.78m), Myers 5ft 10in (1.78m) and Le Saux 5ft 10in (1.78m). Surely any team would go over the top.

Barnsley didn't. But either side of Chelsea's first goal, old boy Darren Barnard nearly scored. The tidy left-sided player, who didn't make a major impression at Stamford Bridge, skipped past Wise and Di Matteo and was only foiled by de Goey's long whipped out hand as he tried to go round the goalkeeper, and then his thirty-yard high-riser was dramatically punched over by de Goey. The big goalkeeper was laying down his credentials to the team now.

Apart from that it was just a glorious Chelsea afternoon, and after the first two goals it was the Gianluca Vialli show.

Dan Petrescu opens the scoring

Barnsley

Watson

Eaden Moses De Zeeuw Barnard

Tinkler

Redfearn Sheridan
(Marcelle 46)

Bullock

Hendrie Wilkinson
(Liddell 59) (Hristov 46)

Referee: Graham Poll (Herts)

Zola Vialli
(Flo 54)

Di Matteo

Poyet Petrescu
(Nicholls 69) (Granville 71)

Wise

Le Saux Myers Clarke Sinclair

de Goey

Chelsea

Goal 1: Petrescu took advantage of the total mess in Barnsley's area as Wise's tantalizing cross was misheaded by Eaden and hooked nowhere in particular by De Zeeuw. 'Ledge' Petrescu dummied to shoot, stepped inside Moses, and calmly left-footed the ball in off the post.

Goal 2: Vialli and Wise set up Sinclair on the right, he used Wise's run outside as a decoy to cut inside, and his left-foot cross found Poyet unmarked at the far post. Poyet's downward header was blocked by goalkeeper Watson, but the Chelsea man stabbed home the rebound. His first goal for his new club, and the celebratory laughter was clearly his signature.

Goal 3: One of the goals of the season. De Goey caught a Barnsley corner and launched a magnificent throw out to Petrescu on the halfway line wide on the left. Petrescu had run there diagonally, and now he took one touch before driving a wonderful pass forward to Vialli who was running diagonally the other way. There seemed no access as Vialli reached the penalty area shadowed by Moses, but he unleashed an extraordinary half-volley when the ball caught up with him, and it shot round the defender and goalkeeper and went in at the near post.

Goal 4: Substitute Flo won the ball off the bemused De Zeeuw, Poyet took it up and chipped over Moses. Vialli's first shot was blocked by Watson but he recovered to head home off the bar.

Goal 5: Vialli's hat-trick. Brilliant one-touch play. Di Matteo hared through the middle, slipped the ball right to Poyet, who squared it left to Wise. Wise could have shot but slipped it wide to Vialli in space on the left, and he placed it across the goalkeeper.

Goal 6: Vialli's fourth. Wise's outswinging corner was headed on by Clarke into the penalty area. Watson could only punch it quickly beyond the goal to where Vialli stood alone. He belted it back, left foot, first touch.

Wise, who last season had worn a T-shirt with the slogan 'Cheer up Luca, we love you, xxx' for perennial substitute Vialli, now said: 'When Luca got his hat-trick goal he just turned round and said: "I'm so lucky." I asked him after the match: "What you on about? 'I'm so lucky'!" He said: "I had five chances and scored four goals." And at the time he'd had three chances and scored three. I said: "Nah, you're not lucky. It's called good finishing." And on that fifth chance I think he was just being unselfish because when he was through he seemed to be trying to get the defender to score an own goal.'

In fact that final effort was an embarrassing slice, but it didn't matter then. Chelsea had announced their arrival in the championship race. The only downers were Zola's quiet performance and Wise's third booking in three games, a harsh decision for a challenge which didn't even look a foul. Six–nil away from home! What a year this could be.

> ❝ I've been very lucky during pre-season, I've always been healthy. I've been working very hard, so now I'm fitter than last year at this time. But now it's very difficult to play in Chelsea because there are four strikers, and Mark, Gianfranco and Flo are all good players. So when you get the chance you have to score and play as well as possible because it's not easy to change the manager's mind. ❞
>
> Gianluca Vialli

	Barnsley	Chelsea
Shots on target	4	8
Corners	4	7
Fouls	7	13
Offsides	5	7
Bookings	0	1
Wise, foul (88 mins).		

	Barnsley	Chelsea
Goals	0	6
Petrescu (25), Poyet (37), Vialli (43, 56, 63, 81)		
Assists		
Sinclair, De Goey, Petrescu, Poyet (2), Wise, Di Matteo		

Wednesday 27 August
Selhurst Park
22,237

Wimbledon 0 Chelsea 2

SIXTH PLACE, FOUR POINTS BEHIND LEADERS, GAME IN HAND

Michael Duberry snapped his achilles tendon in training on Thursday 16 January. The serious injury has slowed down top international footballers like Neil Webb and John Barnes and tapered off their careers.

But Duberry was far younger when he suffered his blow, and there was little doubt that he would make a full recovery. An England Under-21s regular, a hot tip for a full international future, his rise from the basement of reserve team player to Chelsea's plum property had been exhilaratingly quick.

He had hoped to make pre-season training, but the club was taking no risks with his fitness. He was given all the time he needed. He did a lot of running but didn't join in the football.

When ready, he started training with the youth team. Then, two weeks before the game at Wimbledon, he moved back to training with the first team. The following Monday he played forty-five minutes for the reserves in an Avon Insurance Combination League game. On the Thursday he managed forty-five minutes in a friendly at the training ground against China.

He looked not bad at all. The following Tuesday he was drafted into the first team squad, and against the direct football of Wimbledon, he returned to the top drawer.

It wasn't easy. Since the end of his first year as a trainee he had played in a back three. Now he was asked to adjust to a back four.

Ruud Gullit said later: 'Michael Duberry was surprised to play.

Chelsea cool: *Petrescu, Poyet, Di Matteo, Wise and Duberry celebrate Di Matteo's goal*

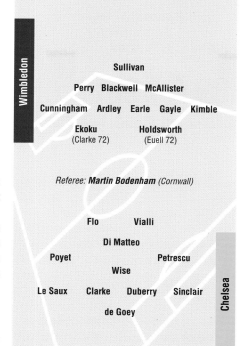

Wimbledon

Sullivan

Perry   Blackwell   McAllister

Cunningham   Ardley   Earle   Gayle   Kimble

Ekoku   Holdsworth
(Clarke 72)   (Euell 72)

*Referee: **Martin Bodenham** (Cornwall)*

Flo   Vialli

Di Matteo

Poyet   Petrescu

Wise

Le Saux   Clarke   Duberry   Sinclair

de Goey

Chelsea

He was not fit but he didn't have to run much because Wimbledon look to knock the ball back at you.'

Chelsea were such a major influence in the land that Wimbledon became the third team in three Premiership games to change their normal game plan for the challenge. Coventry normally played with a back four, but used a man-marker on Zola and switched to a back three. Barnsley had played two games with a back three but switched to a back four to try and defend in numbers. Wimbledon switched from a back four to a back three to try and combat us in midfield.

But maybe they had plans to man-mark Zola too. It was a waste of time. He wasn't selected.

The impressive Flo got his full debut partnering the prolific Vialli up front and, as in the semi-final the previous season, Chelsea's change of tactics was too much for Wimbledon.

Following the stupidity of Coventry and the swagger of Barnsley, Chelsea supplied an impressively professional performance at Wimbledon.

Flo missed an early chance when he scuffed his shot after Duberry's tackle had allowed Wise to send Di Matteo away on a great run. All the same, goalkeeper Sullivan had to dive to save.

Just before half-time Petrescu's

header from Sinclair's shot bulleted straight into Sullivan.

In between time, big Duberry sailed through affairs and Wimbledon's only chance came when de Goey scuffed a clearance and Holdsworth shot lamely back. Duberry's size and athleticism were definitely an advantage, however short his fitness.

Wimbledon have never been good starters to the season, and Chelsea have long had a good record at their ground. In the second-half the story was the same, and although Gayle whacked one over after Poyet had lost possession, it was no surprise when Chelsea took the lead. It was Di Matteo's first special of the campaign, a sizzling twenty-five-yarder just before the hour. He celebrated with his foot up, armchair style, and everyone joined in.

Four minutes later the match was won. Le Saux and Vialli combined to feed Flo on the left, and the striker strode round the back of the defence and along the by-line before cutting the ball back for the unmarked Petrescu to pick his spot. It was like a needle weaving through cloth.

Wimbledon had only one shot in the whole of the second-half, and that was well off target. A second clean sheet running, a few rested players, a new player's debut and a (young) old favourite returning. A good night's work.

	Wimbledon	Chelsea
Shots on target	1	6
Corners	7	6
Fouls	7	9
Offsides	10	5
Bookings	2	3

Holdsworth on Clarke (67 mins); McAllister on Vialli (72); Clarke, foul (1); Le Saux, foul (84); Petrescu, dissent (86).

> *Who in the world would have guessed that after the way Hughes and Zola performed last year, that they would not be playing at Wimbledon? Tore and Luca played very well and we deserved our victory. That's a squad system. Zola tore Wimbledon apart in the semi-final and over at their place in the League a few days later. As I walked along the touchline before the game, I looked over to their management as you do and said: "Alright, Joe." And Joe Kinnear said: "Where the **** is Zola?" They had worked hard for days to stop Zola playing.*
>
> Graham Rix

	Wimbledon	Chelsea
Goals	0	2

Di Matteo (59), Petrescu (63)

Assists
Flo

Saturday 30 August
Stamford Bridge
30,008

Chelsea 4 Southampton 2

NEW STAND, FULL GROUND, GREAT ATMOSPHERE

In November 1995 the North Stand, since renamed the Matthew Harding Stand, was opened, the first stadium development since the East Stand was finally finished in 1974. Twenty-one years of decay came to an end.

Now, less than two years later, the other end of the ground was finished. Welcome to the Shed Umbro Stand incorporating the Family Centre in the lower tier and the Galleria, a long room the width of the pitch, under the upper tier.

It looked fresh and clean, it was close to the pitch and, in the sunshine, it was simply brilliant. The fans went wild.

The dreadful old West Stand was gone too, and the lower tier

There were teething problems, of course, but when the injured Newton carried the FA Cup onto the pitch minutes before kick-off the buzz exploded into a wonderful frenzy. Chelsea and silverware was the rarest of marriages.

'When Wise went up to lift the FA Cup, we were there, we were there …' everyone sang.

Cool Eddie, scorer of that perfect second goal at Wembley, raised the trophy at all corners of the ground. Ruud Gullit, sexy football, new signings, masses of away goals, reborn ground, in Europe … no wonder there wasn't a seat to spare.

And for forty-five minutes the football was as perfect as anyone

Hughes bows to the Shed after heading Chelsea's third

of the new development was running the length of the pitch, from the Shed to the Matthew Harding, with seats most of the way – from penalty area to penalty area.

For the first time you could sense what Stamford Bridge might become. And the team was so exciting. There was unfettered optimism everywhere.

could have dreamed.

There had been just one scare before Chelsea took the lead after six minutes. De Goey and then Le Saux had both bravely blocked after young Davies had latched onto Leboeuf's poor header. The fit again Leboeuf had returned for the rested Clarke – the squad system once more at work.

de Goey

Sinclair   Duberry   Leboeuf   Le Saux

Wise

Petrescu   Poyet
(Clarke 78)

Di Matteo
(Nicholls 70)

M Hughes   Zola
(Vialli 70)

*Referee: **Alan Wilkie** (Chester-le-Street)*

Ostenstad   Davies
(Evans 48)

Spedding   Maddison   Magilton   D Hughes
(Williams 71) (Neilson 48)

Todd   Benali   Monkou   Dodd

Jones

Southampton

The goal climaxed a marvellous period of keep-ball. Play opened up with Zola's crossfield pass, and then the tight intricacies of Petrescu, Sinclair and Wise, back-flicks and all, resulted in Petrescu accelerating away from a challenge and chipping a beautiful twenty-yard lob over the goggled-eyed Jones.

The more Southampton pushed tight on Chelsea, the more the one-touch football destroyed them. This wasn't pass and move, this was pass and fly.

Just before the half hour farce dragged Southampton level. De Goey took a third touch on a pass back and Davies closed him down and blocked his clearance. It bounced back into the net.

Southampton then caved in to Chelsea's relentless forward pressure. Poyet enjoyed a free header from Zola's corner, and although Todd chested off the line Leboeuf forced the ball in. Hughes was left free to stoop and dive at Le Saux's measured cross, sending a powerful header over Jones. Zola turned Benali inside out in the penalty area, spinning outside, inside, running his foot over the ball before slipping it to Petrescu. Poor Spedding, trying to cover, squared it across his own penalty area where the laughing Wise slipped it in. Three goals in six minutes in front of the ecstatic Shed. Four–one at half-time.

Unfortunately Chelsea rested throughout the second-half. A couple of near misses early on were followed by de Goey stretching on the edge of his box to stop Ostenstad, and then being beaten by Chelsea old boy Monkou who took advantage of a tiring Duberry to chest down a long ball and finish like a forward. He never did that at Chelsea.

Midway through the half Poyet smashed a volley against the post to show that Chelsea were only sleeping, but unnecessary sourness entered proceedings when Sinclair allowed himself to be riled by an irritating Williams who subsequently collapsed to the ground when the Chelsea man raised his arm. It seemed an injustice when Sinclair was sent off, but you don't raise your arms. Considering he had been fined £750 for his 'dropping the shorts' celebration when he scored against Coventry, it was turning into an up-and-down season for him.

But, in general, Chelsea life was on an unbelievable high.

> *I'm feeling quite strong. I made two bursts in the last twenty minutes and that's quite good for me. I've not cramped up so far. I hadn't had a full ninety minutes before Wimbledon, so I'm pleased with myself.*
>
> **Michael Duberry**

> *The most important thing was the second-half. You have to be focused for the whole game. It's understandable you get a bit less concerned after a 4–1 lead, but it's important you don't get sloppy. Overall it was a good win. When we were with ten men we were in control of the game because at that moment everybody's focused again.*
>
> **Ruud Gullit**

	Chelsea	Southampton
Shots on target	8	1
Woodwork	1	0
Corners	6	9
Fouls	4	14
Offsides	7	6
Bookings	0	4

Monkou on Zola (66), Benali on Vialli (80); D Hughes on Duberry (81), Williams on Duberry (85).

	Chelsea	Southampton
Sending off	1	0

Sinclair, raising arm (78).

	Chelsea	Southampton
Goals	4	2

Petrescu (6), Leboeuf (27), M Hughes (30), Wise (33); Davies (24), Monkou 58)

Assists

Poyet, Le Saux, Zola

Saturday 13 September
Selhurst Park
26,186

Crystal Palace 0 Chelsea 3
INTERNATIONALS MIDWEEK, SQUAD WIN AT WEEKEND

A midweek Italy game in which Di Matteo and Zola were involved persuaded Ruud Gullit to play without all three of his Italians for the first time since they had joined. Sinclair was suspended following the sending off against Southampton and Clarke had torn a calf muscle in training, so Paul Hughes was thrown in at right-back. His entire previous experience there had come in forty-five minutes of a pre-season friendly at West Bromwich Albion. Maybe the squad wasn't as strong as we'd believed.

Another youngster given his chance on the day was Mark Nicholls, in place of Di Matteo. A prolific goalscoring youth team player, Nicholls had yet to show the pace or strength to play in the front line at senior level, but towards the end of the previous season had shone in an attacking midfield role. Now his impressive pre-season form was rewarded.

Newly promoted Palace, Division One play-off winners thanks to a last-minute wonder goal from Chelsea old boy David Hopkin, had sold their matchwinner to Leeds for £3.25 million. They were giving a home debut to Neil Emblen, just purchased from Wolves, and they were struggling to find more than a handful of Premiership-quality players.

If Chelsea had Championship potential, this was a game they simply ought to win.

They did. And once again they did it with panache and cool.

Hughes and Nicholls slotted in with ease, the pass and fly movement continued and Palace, who couldn't win at home, quickly died.

Former Chelsea youngster Neil Shipperley, now Palace's centre-forward, moaned: 'It was like playing against eighteen men. Wherever you looked there were Chelsea players.'

And old Blues midfielder Ray Lewington, now Palace's coach, admitted: 'Chelsea knew they had a little bit too much for us, were generally just keeping the ball, and I think we annoyed them in the last minute and they smacked another one in.'

Three weeks earlier, on the same ground, Wimbledon's plans

Hughes volleys Lebouef's fifty-yard pass to open the scoring

Miller

Tuttle   Roberts   Linighan

Muscat   Emblen   Fullarton   Gordon
(Zohar 73)   (Veart 82)

Lombardo

Shipperley   Dyer
(Freedman 55)

Referee: **Gerald Ashby** (Worcester)

M Hughes   Flo

Nicholls

Poyet   Petrescu

Wise

Le Saux   Clarke   Duberry   P Hughes

de Goey

Chelsea

had been thrown into disarray when Zola didn't play. Now Palace manager Steve Coppell seemed to believe that plans were irrelevant. 'I've got their team sheet knocking around in my pocket. and when you look at their substitutes, you think: "Oh ****" – the last thing you want to do is get in front. Well, there wasn't much chance of that. They are excellent. They worked harder to win the ball back than they did when they were in possession, and that's the quality of their team. In possession, each and every one of them is comfortable, they run off the ball so well, they receive the ball so well. But those sort of players cost a fortune to assemble and they earn their wages.'

Mark Hughes picked up an early booking for checking Linighan and Palace actually worked the first good opening, Dyer leaving Le Saux on his backside and crossing from the by-line, but de Goey cleared.

Chelsea, however, created chance after chance, and Miller saved bravely at the feet of Hughes and Flo, but after nineteen minutes Hughes made a wonderful run with a change of direction which was picked out by Leboeuf's stunning fifty-yard pass. As Miller raced from his goal Hughes jabbed the ball past him first touch on the stretch volley. One-nil.

Five minutes later, with Dyer heading badly over from Gordon's cross in the meantime, Petrescu received Wise's fine pass, played a mesmerizingly quick one-two with Hughes to get in the box and was dragged back by Linighan. Leboeuf blasted in the penalty.

Miller made a double save from Nicholls and Hughes, but was beaten again just before half-time when Le Saux took Poyet's clever switch-of-play pass and hammered an eighteen-yarder high against the near post. It nearly broke!

The second-half was the same. Flo wasted Wise's wonderful fifty-yard pass after the captain had beaten two men, Miller blocked again from Hughes and Poyet, and Chelsea lorded it.

Then, suddenly, with just over twenty minutes left Palace substitute Freedman got in behind the left side of defence, was one on one with de Goey, and hit a fierce low drive which the goalkeeper dropped down to with superb agility and palmed away.

Palace's weak hopes died, and in the last minute Chelsea scored a wonderful goal to make the scoreline as impressive as the performance. Le Saux charged past Poyet as Wise played a crossfield ball, Poyet intelligently hooked it on first time, and Le Saux's strike this time blasted in off the inside post. He went nuts celebrating his first goal since his return to Chelsea. 'He got a little bit carried away and we got a bit embarrassed for him. We let him get on with it because he looked rather stupid. He was like a little kid who'd just scored his first goal,' said Wise as the left-back jumped and bounded across the pitch, arms raised.

Later, as Wise left a happy dressing room, Di Matteo looked up from his bench coolly. 'Wisey! It was a pleasure playing with you.'

It had been a pleasure for everyone.

	Crystal Palace	Chelsea
Shots on target	2	8
Woodwork	0	1
Corners	3	7
Fouls	10	11
Offsides	5	9
Bookings	2	3

Linighan not withdrawing ten yards (16), Tuttle on M Hughes (29), Muscat, squaring up to Poyet (35); M Hughes, foul (4), Poyet, squaring up (35).

> **I have a feeling with Sparky since our first season. I know the ball he likes and I know how he runs. I see him running in a special side, and I say: "Okay, I will do this," and I try to put the ball there. I saw the ball coming to Sparky. I didn't expect he would turn and shoot. But it was beautiful. It was amazing.**
>
> Frank Leboeuf

	Crystal Palace	Chelsea
Goals	0	3

M Hughes (19), Leboeuf (pen) (24), Le Saux (90)

Assists

Leboeuf, Petrescu, Wise, Poyet

Thursday 18 September
Stamford Bridge
23,067

Chelsea 2 Slovan Bratislava 0

PERFECT, PATIENT EUROPEAN LAUNCH

Wonderful so far, but let's face it, Chelsea were winning games they would be expected to win. The wonderful part was that these had been not only wins but massacres. The football was a dream.

Much had advanced since last season. There was the subtlety of Poyet, the improvement from Sinclair, the return of Duberry. But more than anything there was the form of Wise.

In the absence of the injured anchor midfielder Newton, Wise had added the defensive discipline to his game to become a midfield general. There were a few surges into attack, there was constant covering and support, and although he didn't have the dexterity and pace of an in-form Newton to do the complete

skillful, two-footed, can pass with his left or right easily and he works well in small spaces.'

Slovan had pedigree. Regular European competitors, they were the only other team apart from Chelsea in this year's European Cup Winners' Cup to have won it. They did that in 1969, two years before Chelsea.

They had come third in the Slovakian League the previous season. They had earnt their place in the first round by beating Bulgaria's Levski Sofia, themselves no push-overs, in the preliminaries.

Sinclair was again suspended, this time because of a booking in Chelsea's last European game three seasons before. Le Saux was

Di Matteo strikes Chelsea's first European goal of the season

defensive midfield job, his vision and passing had become the ignition to the team. There was less defending to do than for a long time because Chelsea had possession for so much of the game.

Gullit was in no doubt. 'Dennis was outstanding again at Crystal Palace and I think he aims once more for the national team. It's a different role for him and I think his performances depend on many things. I think he has improved technically a lot. He's very

also suspended after a European punch-up with his own player, Batty, at Blackburn. Paul Hughes continued at right-back and Granville returned for his eighth Chelsea appearance. It was to be a momentous one.

Sadly, the stadium was far from full. The decision to make this a Category A game – top prices – allied to the match being broadcast live on television, seemed to keep people away.

Chelsea

de Goey

P Hughes Duberry Leboeuf Granville

Wise

Petrescu   Poyet

Di Matteo

Vialli Zola

Referee: **Roberto Boggi** (Italy)

Borisenko
(Muzlay 62)

Gunda Kereszturi Tomaschek Sobona Novak
(Moder 80)   (Timko 50)

Antalovic Glonek Pecko

Hornyak

Konig

Slovan Bratislava

What a shame, because this was such an absorbing game. Not exhilarating, as the previous League games had been, but an intelligent European encounter.

Gullit matched Vialli and Zola up front for the first time in the season. Hornyak man-marked Zola but came off second best. Chelsea had all the possession and all the shots, but the goals did not mount up.

It started so well. Paul Hughes' ball into the edge of the box was worked by Zola and Petrescu to Di Matteo who rifled in accurately from fifteen yards for his first ever European goal. Only five minutes had gone.

Ignition complete. But the blast-off never followed. It didn't matter at first, but as time ate away at the spirit, it began to be a worry.

Zola whipped a free-kick from the left touchline against the bar and a minute later Vialli missed the target from six yards. Konig palmed away Zola's left-footer after brilliant interplay with Vialli, and then the goalkeeper couldn't hold Wise's twenty-five-yarder but was rescued by his defence. Half an hour gone.

Vialli turned his man but shot against the near post, and later turned his man again but Poyet just couldn't

reach his cross when a touch would have done. Zola's angled shot was kept out by Konig. Half-time. It was okay, one up, but you wanted another goal from such domination.

The second-half was the same. The crowd started it by singing but gradually grew quiet and tense. If only one more would go in.

Di Matteo shot straight at Konig from close range after Zola had touched on Petrescu's cross. Konig was stretched by another Wise twenty-five-yarder. On and on came Chelsea. Slovan were stretched and they suffered three bookings in eight minutes. But the ball wouldn't go in.

Granville stole forward but just couldn't respond to Wise's deflected shot and was blocked. Zola and Petrescu wove magic for Vialli to exercise an overhead effort which was blocked, and from the rebound Poyet beat the defender but blazed over. Fifteen minutes to go.

Slowly, slowly, the hope was being drained from the crowd. Quieter, edgier. What if Slovan broke clear?

With eleven minutes left Paul Hughes crossed a somewhat innocuous ball into the box. Granville had stolen forward again, and with amazing skill he flicked it back from the defender, then sideways over the defender's head before dodging round him to volley home before the ball dropped. An amazing first goal for the club he joined on transfer deadline week the season before.

His knees-up, arms-up celebration became the laughing stock of his colleagues for weeks to come. They called him Karate Kid. Gullit celebrated Granville's first touch as the product of the half hour's work on technique most players put in before training each day.

The last ten minutes were fine. The fact that Slovan hadn't got a sniff at 1–0 was irrelevant. At 2–0 it was proof of Chelsea's domination. At the final whistle it was a fourth clean sheet in five games.

	Chelsea	S Bratislava
Shots on target	11	1
Woodwork	2	0
Corners	8	3
Fouls	15	17
Offsides	4	2
Bookings	1	4

P Hughes, foul(56); Tomaschek on Wise (33), Sobona on Leboeuf (53), Antalovic on Vialli (56); Timko on Granville (61).

> *I was behind him. After he flicked the ball over the defender's head I could see by his face, it was so concentrated. I was sure he was going to score. Great goal. He stayed calm when he shot. Really very good.*
>
> **Gianfranco Zola on Granville**

	Chelsea	Southampton
Goals	4	2

Di Matteo (5), Granville (79).

Assists
Zola, Petrescu

Sunday 21 September
Stamford Bridge
31,549

Chelsea 2 Arsenal 3
FIRST DESERVED DEFEAT OF SEASON

Chelsea third, Arsenal fourth, and Chelsea with a game in hand. Arsenal's Bergkamp the individual revelation of the season so far. Chelsea's football the team revelation of the season.

During the week Arsenal had got it wrong in Europe again, losing in Greece in the UEFA Cup. Now the questions revolved around how well Chelsea could recover from a Thursday European home game, and how they would fare against a top-quality side.

Gullit kept faith with Vialli and Zola, and continued with Paul Hughes at right-back even though he would now be up against an international winger. Arsenal had problems with Adams' fitness and Wright's loss of form.

And by the end of another unnecessarily bad-tempered game between top sides, mirroring the Charity Shield, Chelsea had suffered a sending off, a cruel injury and a late defeat.

Bergkamp stood out from the beginning. Chelsea's defending was in panic as he twice ran through them in the first half-hour but couldn't find the finish.

Just once in the first-half Chelsea managed that swagger that had characterized the season so far. The move started down the left with Le Saux finding Vialli who turned Adams and crossed well. Zola chested the ball down for Poyet to shoot, and Bould blocked at full stretch.

But at the other end Parlour went on a great run past Wise and

Poyet and the Family Centre hail his goal

The West Stand seats were spreading further along the lower tier bringing more people in. Live on television, everything was set for another swaggering performance laced with genius.

It never came. The game was poor. Both teams looked tired. It wasn't lack of confidence or intent. Both were determined not to lose and both seemed to think that they could win. But both laboured.

Le Saux and crossed for Overmars who volleyed over. Arsenal were having the better of things without being convincing.

The real action started in the last fifteen minutes of the first half. Leboeuf was booked for a late challenge on Bergkamp just outside the Chelsea penalty area as the Dutchman turned cleverly again. But Parlour escaped any caution when kicking Le Saux up the backside after the ball had run away from both of them.

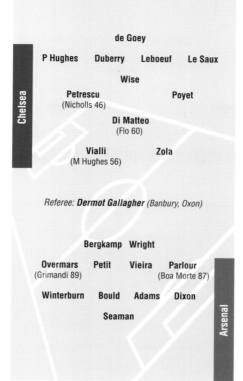

de Goey

P Hughes   **Duberry**   **Leboeuf**   **Le Saux**

Wise

Petrescu   **Poyet**
(Nicholls 46)

Di Matteo
(Flo 60)

Vialli   **Zola**
(M Hughes 56)

Chelsea

Referee: **Dermot Gallagher** (Banbury, Oxon)

Bergkamp   Wright

Overmars   **Petit**   **Vieira**   **Parlour**
(Grimandi 89)   (Boa Morte 87)

Winterburn   **Bould**   **Adams**   **Dixon**

Seaman

Arsenal

Tempers flared all round. Tackles grew ugly and referee Dermot Gallagher lost some control.

Chelsea's refusal to lose confidence led to them stealing the opening goal. Vialli took a quick short corner to Wise, and Wise's early cross was misheaded by Duberry across a static Adams to the predatory Poyet who hooked it in. The Stamford Bridge crowd exploded. Poyet jumped like a jack-in-the-box, he laughed like a hyena and he buried himself deep in the hearts of all Chelsea fans. What a character.

Going forward Chelsea could afford to retain confidence. But at the back it wasn't so easy. Midfielder Paul Hughes stuck to his right-back task as best he could, but Overmars was quick if not often deadly.

Right on half-time Chelsea cracked. Duberry failed to clear far enough upfield and was left struggling when Vieira chipped back. Wright nodded on, Bergkamp raced clear, everyone else was nowhere. The lead had lasted five minutes.

Petrescu was unwell at half-time so Nicholls came on. Wise started the second-half with a twenty-five-yarder which Seaman needed two attempts to save, and a savage challenge on Vieira which earnt him his fourth yellow card in eight games.

Bergkamp continued to dominate. His free-kick was headed wide by Bould and his volley a minute later was palmed away by de Goey.

Gullit sent on Mark Hughes for Vialli and two minutes later Bergkamp scored again after more defensive errors. Wright

lobbed Le Saux on the edge of the area, Duberry and Leboeuf got in each other's way, clearing only to Bergkamp who calmly drove home.

Yet two minutes later Chelsea's resolve not to lose flowered again. Hughes moved wide, Leboeuf picked him out once more with a perfect long pass, and his cross evaded Adams and a badly flailing Seaman to give the tip-toeing Zola his first goal of the season. Dreadful Arsenal defending, but who cared.

Clearly Chelsea could win. Gullit sent on Flo for Di Matteo to play with three up. Five minutes later Bould was booked for fouling him from behind. Another minute later and Leboeuf tripped Bergkamp on the surge, his second bookable offence, and he was off.

Problems! Three attackers, no midfield or defence. But Poyet went to centre-half and was superb. Zola and Hughes took turns to work like terriers in midfield. Chelsea clung on. Supporters of both teams were going wild. Time and again Overmars ran at Paul Hughes, but he stayed stubborn, if not resistant. Chelsea seemed to be heading for a draw when with two minutes left Winterburn launched an unstoppable thirty-yarder into the top corner. He was one player too many to close down. Sickeningly for Chelsea, he celebrated in front of his own fans.

There was still time for Arsenal to pick up two more bookings in a bad-tempered last minute, and right on time substitute Boa Morte launched himself at Duberry, landing agonizingly on his ankle, yet escaped a whistle. As the players left the pitch Duberry was writhing in agony, and his torn ligaments would take two months to repair.

	Chelsea	Arsenal
Shots on target	4	7
Corners	5	3
Fouls	17	22
Offsides	5	5
Bookings	1	3

Wise, foul (46); Bould on Flo (65), Bergkamp on Le Saux (90), Grimandi on Le Saux (90).
Sending off
Leboeuf, two bookings, fouls (34) and (66)

> *They didn't recover well from the Thursday game. Too many people were not fit, not tuned in. The main moment was when we scored, 2–2. We could go for more and I put Flo on. Then Leboeuf got sent off and ruins your plans and you have too many strikers. If you saw how Zola and Mark Hughes battled, and also Poyet, it was incredible.*
>
> **Ruud Gullit**

	Chelsea	Arsenal
Goals	2	3

Poyet (39), Zola (59); Bergkamp (44, 58), Winterburn (88)

Assists
Wise, Duberry, Leboeuf, M Hughes

Wednesday 24 September
Old Trafford
55,163

Manchester United 2 Chelsea 2

JUST TWO DEFEATS IN LAST TWENTY-THREE LEAGUE VISITS TO OLD TRAFFORD

The super-tense highwire atmosphere was taking over the big games completely. It wasn't necessarily affecting the football which tonight was wonderful, but it was spoiling the spectacle.

It certainly marred this one. Chelsea arrived at Old Trafford full of the confidence that their record there ensured. Ten wins and ten draws in the last twenty-two League games. But United, inevitably, were top of the League.

Di Matteo was missing with a broken finger. Lambourde, back from a nasty pre-season hip injury, made his debut in an unfamiliar role in midfield, and Chelsea lined up for the first time in the season with an almost flat midfield four. With Duberry and Clarke both injured Myers played centre-back and was immaculate.

corners. Pass and fly, pass and fly.

Lambourde won the ball off Butt and Petrescu fed Hughes for a shot which forced Schmeichel to the first of several excellent saves. He parried and Poyet just couldn't direct the rebound in.

Lambourde generally adjusted well, playing simply, control and pass, but every so often he got caught out by the pace, and found himself yellow carded after just eight minutes for pulling back Keane.

Paul Hughes headed out excellently from Cole under pressure to show he was adjusting to his role, and after twenty-three minutes Chelsea bizarrely took the lead. Le Saux stepped inside a defender and fired a twenty-five-yarder which Schmeichel again parried, but the ball bounced back off the astonished Berg over his own keeper and in. Chelsea were in the lead at Old Trafford again, and in this

Mark Hughes, Zola and Poyet congratulate Le Saux on his assist for the own goal

United's crowd has always tended to go quiet if they aren't leading after twenty minutes. This was no different. But this was a night in which, ultimately, no-one could stay quiet.

Within forty seconds Scholes had headed wide after a swift United interchange. In the first four minutes Chelsea won two

twenty-three-year run the top scorer was now 'o.g.' with five.

Chelsea were confident and began to get on top. Wise's pass dissected Neville and Beckham for Le Saux to cross, but Hughes' header was well blocked by Pallister. Then the move of the game: Leboeuf won the ball, passed forward to Hughes whose incredible

Manchester United

Schmeichel

G Neville   Pallister   Berg   Irwin
(Giggs 78)

Beckham   Keane   Butt   Poborsky
                                    (Sheringham 60)

Scholes   Cole
(Solskjaer 60)

*Referee: **Gary Willard** (Worthing)*

M Hughes   Zola
                (Flo 88)

Poyet   Wise   Lambourde   Petrescu

Le Saux   Myers   Leboeuf   P Hughes

de Goey

Chelsea

lay-off to Poyet was followed by a turn and run by the striker. Poyet passed to Zola whose unbelievable first-time smack of the ball landed it right in Hughes' path. His drive was brilliantly saved.

Three minutes before the half hour the bad tempers exploded. Keane, who had caught Poyet in the head at Wembley, kicked him up the backside viciously. He escaped with a yellow card.

Ten minutes before half-time Poborsky on the left wing was judged to be not interfering with play as he came back from an offside position and the ball was played up towards him. Chelsea stopped, Cole raced away and fed Scholes who equalized.

Chelsea went mad, surrounding the linesman and the referee. Even the normally laid-back Gullit was on his feet lecturing the linesman and pointing at him. The officials' decision looked clearly wrong. Those kind of decisions at Old Trafford are bound to incense visitors. Now the explosion was spreading.

United went forward more penetratingly, confident and impressive. Chelsea countered, furious. Scholes was booked for kicking at Petrescu, Keane raised his arms at Myers but referee Gary Willard reached for his card, realized the situation and changed his mind. Keane thus escaped a sending off. Chelsea grew more furious.

Pallister headed a cracker from Beckham's free-kick against the bar, Zola and Wise were booked right on half-time for a slide tackle and the raising of an arm at Beckham respectively. Beckham dropped immediately, holding his face, and more mayhem broke out. Wise booked, Keane not so. Wise would now be suspended as a result.

When the teams went off they took their arguments into the tunnel.

The second-half continued to see Chelsea the more impressive. Petrescu forced another great Schmeichel save after being set up by Zola, and on sixty-three minutes the Blues scored again. De Goey's throw was carried by Paul Hughes to the halfway line, Petrescu took it forward and crossed where Schmeichel did a 'Seaman' from Sunday, missed the low effort and allowed Hughes to score against his old club.

Substitute Sheringham missed a great chance to equalize when he smashed over, and Lambourde should have wrapped it up when he burst through on a one-two with Hughes but his first touch let him down and Schmeichel blocked. Leggy Lambourde's physical contribution had been right on the night.

The bookings kept coming and with five minutes to go, with Chelsea looking safe, two points were thrown away. Mark Hughes lost possession in his own half, and when the ball was crossed in Leboeuf's sliced header took the ball away from Paul Hughes to Solskjaer. The substitute curled in an amazing equalizer. The defending was a carbon copy of the losing goal conceded at Coventry.

In the last minute a bruised but business-like United nearly nicked all three points, Cole being given space to angle a shot which de Goey dropped on.

Four goals, eight bookings, one suspension, countless bruises and scratches. Another Old Trafford without defeat, so plenty to laugh about. But no-one was laughing.

	Man Utd	Chelsea
Shots on target	4	6
Woodwork	1	0
Corners	5	3
Fouls	20	14
Offsides	3	8
Bookings	3	5

Keane on Poyet (27), Scholes on Petrescu (38), Irwin on Petrescu (63); Lambourde foul (8), Zola, foul (44), Wise, raising arm (45), P Hughes, foul (78), M Hughes, dissent (81).

❜ I think Chelsea are too good a side to give starts like that. They've come here in the past and defended, caught us on the counter, things like that. But this team's got more than previous Chelsea teams. ❜

Alex Ferguson

	Man Utd	Chelsea
Goals	2	2

Scholes (35), Solskjaer (85); Berg o.g. (23), M Hughes (67)

Assists

Le Saux, Petrescu

Saturday 27 September
Stamford Bridge
31,563

Chelsea 1 Newcastle United 0

FROM CHAMPIONS TO RUNNERS-UP

Ruudi decided to lay down the law. He wasn't having Frank Sinclair waltz back from suspension and straight into the team, so he continued with Paul Hughes. It turned out to be one game too many for the youngster grappling with his new position. But that wasn't really the issue.

Chelsea had taken one point out of six against two of the top teams. Newcastle were lower down the table but with games in hand and were doing better than expected without their injured or sold forwards.

The game started disastrously. Hughes wasn't coping and on the opposite flank Le Saux was having a nightmare. Every time the England left-back played the ball forward he skied it to a Newcastle player.

It took just twenty-four minutes for Gullit to ditch his morals in search of victory, and he committed his earliest substitution of the season. Sinclair came on for Hughes. Immediately things improved.

'We gave so many passes away,' he said. 'We were lucky not to be 1–0 down. I couldn't wait to half-time to change. Paul Hughes was just not in the game, but I'm very happy with him. Frankie was a little bit more aggressive, better tuned in.'

It had started after three minutes with Hughes giving the ball away and de Goey doing well to palm away Tomasson's bottom-corner shot. The confidence seemed to drain from Hughes with Sinclair sat on the bench.

Then when, after twenty minutes, he was left exposed by Beresford's quick free-kick for Batty to cross wickedly and

Poyet heads Chelsea's goal

It was too much for Gullit. He was out of his seat and punching the air in frustration. The cool seemed to be being sapped from the dreadlocked manager.

Perhaps he would have liked to have had himself on the bench this once, but he had so far only put himself there against Slovan Bratislava and had yet to play.

Tomasson to head hopelessly wide, Gullit moved to change.

Newcastle had squandered another chance when veteran Rush appeared to be offside but raced away with three men up against one. The one, Myers, did superbly to clear the cross.

Chelsea weren't dead. Flo had a shot deflected wide, Poyet's twenty-five-yarder needed two attempts from Given to catch and

Chelsea

de Goey

P Hughes Leboeuf Myers Le Saux
(Sinclair 24)

Di Matteo Lambourde Wise Poyet
(M Hughes 57)

Flo Zola

Referee: Mike Riley (Leeds)

Newcastle

Rush Tomasson
(Ketsbaia 55)

Beresford Barnes Batty Barton
(Howey 60) (Gillespie 75)

Pistone Albert Peacock Watson

Given

Poyet also shot wide after good work by Zola and Flo.

But after the substitution everything was better and Given became the star of the show. He palmed away Di Matteo's twenty-five-yarder, he palmed up and held Zola's left-footer after the little man had turned Watson, and he saved Di Matteo's twenty-yarder. He was also relieved to see Flo shoot poorly wide after running clear.

This still wasn't vintage Chelsea but it was Chelsea moving in the right direction. It certainly wasn't vintage Newcastle. Out injured were Shearer, Asprilla and Lee. Yet they continued to enjoy chances. Barton sliced wide and three minutes before the interval de Goey came to the rescue again, splendidly palming away Barnes' cross-shot.

There was no doubt that Chelsea were tired. The crowd did everything they could to lift them. But what other football authority would ask their European representative to travel away to the champions midweek between two European legs and then face the runners-up on the Saturday? Worse was to come. It was off to Europe for the second leg next week and then an away journey to Liverpool that weekend.

No wonder Petrescu was taking his turn to rest as the squad continued to rotate. Unfortunately, Di Matteo was out wide again, and he was going through a fallow period.

Leboeuf twice came to Chelsea's rescue early in the second-half, blocking from Barton and tackling Rush. He was having one of his best days. And

although Flo had a shot deflected wide – from the corner Poyet headed just wide – Gullit grew impatient and sent Mark Hughes on for Di Matteo, withdrawing Zola slightly but playing three up front.

It worked. Zola's thirty-yarder flew just past the post, a minute later Flo's diving header from Zola's corner was cleared off the line and Hughes flew in but was blocked as the ball went for another corner. Wise took that one and Poyet rose wonderfully to head home. How he celebrated. Madness! A new hero.

Hughes continued to put Newcastle's defence under pressure, nearly scoring with a cross shot and nearly taking advantage of indecision in their defence. A brilliant move led to Given palming away a dangerous Sinclair cross, but it wouldn't be Chelsea without a final scare.

The wrong-footed de Goey did really well to kick Gillespie's cross shot off the line with a minute left and then, as Newcastle powered forward, Wise's tackle on Pistone was crucial. The captain had again been outstanding.

'We're very tired,' he admitted afterwards. 'We needed to scrape a 1–0 win, we needed to be disciplined. We still gave them a chance at the end, but only one chance. We were bad early on but we still created clear-cut chances.'

Gullit beamed. 'These are the victories that please you the most. I think that in the past Chelsea wouldn't normally win games like this. It would be a draw or also in the last minute a stupid goal.'

It was up to fourth and if the game in hand was won the Blues would be top. Could this really be the year?

> *Today we are together and we played very well defensively except for the first part. The tactic was to wait for Newcastle, to have some space, but we didn't keep the ball when we had it, and it was very difficult to start to play. But we worked, and in the second-half they were very tired and we played great. I was a little bit afraid after our goal because we stopped playing, we tried to keep the score, and if Ed de Goey doesn't save it could be a disaster.*
>
> **Frank Leboeuf**

	Chelsea	Newcastle
Shots on target	10	3
Corners	9	3
Fouls	16	14
Offsides	1	3
Bookings	0	1

Watson on Wise (59).

	Chelsea	Newcastle
Goal	1	0
Poyet (74)		
Assist		
Wise		

Thursday 2 October
Tehelne Pole
13,800

Slovan Bratislava 0 Chelsea 2

CHELSEA WON 4–0 ON AGGREGATE

Fly out Wednesday morning, book into the hotel mid-afternoon, train in the stadium Wednesday evening. The grass was long and Andy Myers sprained a knee ligament and was ruled out. Why do little injuries always catch up with Andy?

Bratislava had a good home European record, but in truth there was nothing to fear here. At Stamford Bridge they had offered nothing coming forward.

So it was time for professionalism but not full throttle. And Sunday at Liverpool had to be considered. Leboeuf would be suspended. Myers had now joined Duberry on the injured list. Clarke may be back by then. Who would play with him?

Slovakian football had not prospered like that of the Czech

Republic after Czechoslovakia had split. And Bratislava was like a provincial city in comparison with Prague, the two capitals of the divorcees.

But Slovakia wasn't standing still. Their national team had just beaten the Czech Republic for the first time. Bratislava was opening up coffee bars everywhere. And you could eat and drink cheaply until the early hours in a basement restaurant, feeling like an old revolutionary.

The players stayed in a city centre hotel opposite the old castle. But the days of them wandering off to see some sites in the hours before the game were long gone. On the Thursday morning they trained again, this time in private. In the afternoon they rested, and

Di Matteo beats Konig for Chelsea's second

Slovan Bratislava

Konig

Pecko Tomaschek Hornyak Gunda

Moder Pukalovic Novak Kereszturi
(Puchner 68)

Muzlay Borisenko
(Nagy 62)

Referee: Alain Hamer (Luxembourg)

Chelsea

Vialli Flo

Di Matteo

Poyet Petrescu
(Babayaro 46) (Nicholls 73)

Wise

Le Saux Leboeuf Lambourde Sinclair
(Granville 64)

de Goey

just a few wandered out of the hotel to stroll up the hill to the castle.

Lambourde, in his unaccustomed midfield role for the last two games, partnered Leboeuf at the back in the evening. Clarke, after not a lot of training, stayed on the substitutes' bench.

In the 32,000 capacity stadium, also the national stadium, UEFA reduced the crowd allowed admission because so much of the ground was terracing. Poor Slovan had passion poured on them behind one goal, but otherwise Chelsea were hardly put upon.

An early goal might have given them confidence, but the one chance they got after twelve minutes was appallingly chipped over by Kereszturi. They were so determined, they committed ten fouls in the first twenty minutes. Gunda shot from a free-kick forty yards out. But they weren't very good.

Midway through the half Chelsea threatened but Gunda's terrific challenge on Petrescu after Vialli's clever pass rescued them. Once more, Gullit was using Vialli in Europe, this time with Flo. The writing on the wall was clear. Zola and Hughes at Liverpool. He was quietly stating priorities.

Chelsea's determination not to concede led to Poyet being booked for a diving challenge on Borisenko, something to put pressure on him for the competition.

Three minutes before the half hour a comfortable Chelsea took the lead. It wasn't a pretty goal but they all count. Di Matteo gracefully accelerated into the penalty area but was dispossessed. The interception was passed back to goalkeeper Konig who hastily kicked clear as Vialli ran in. The ball struck Vialli on the hip as he turned, though everyone else but he claimed it clearly smacked off his backside, and rebounded

in. He didn't mind how it was scored. It was his goal and the tie was over.

Vialli should have had a penalty before the interval when Hornyak pulled him down, but the referee was generous to the home side. A couple of poor de Goey kicks were not taken advantage of, and Lambourde was able to ease through his first game at the back without being tested.

Celestine Babayaro appeared for his debut in the second-half. The record teenage Chelsea signing had suffered a groin strain and stress fracture in the foot during pre-season, but at last was fit. He played in midfield and after just seven minutes cleverly flicked on Leboeuf's long pass for Vialli to run clear. This time Konig did well to deflect his shot against a post.

Di Matteo picked up a booking after Le Saux had lost the ball – every yellow card was met with tense silence from Chelsea fans knowing another in the competition would lead to crucial suspension. But Di Matteo responded well. He had a shot blocked after Konig picked up a back pass and Vialli took a quick free-kick, and then a minute before the hour he scored Chelsea's second. Wise opened the defence up with a diagonal ball, Le Saux turned it inside to Vialli whose cross left Di Matteo alone on the six-yard angle to control and hammer in.

Gullit used the full complement of his three substitutes to keep fresh legs wherever possible. Slovan picked up their first booking of the evening for their twenty-fifth foul after sixty-eight minutes.

Leboeuf had a powerful free-kick brilliantly tipped away by Konig and de Goey athletically turned over a Novak thirty-five-yarder. Chelsea had negotiated a simple visa to the next round.

	S Bratislava	Chelsea
Shots on target	2	4
Woodwork	0	1
Corners	5	4
Fouls	29	13
Offsides	4	4
Bookings	1	2

Pecko on Vialli(68); Poyet, foul (24), Di Matteo, foul (54).

> **You have to be always concentrated. It's vital to start very well, don't give them anything because we know that we can create a lot of chances. We did that, we were lucky because I scored a strange goal. But we deserved to win because we could have scored more goals.**
>
> Gianluca Vialli

	S Bratislava	Chelsea
Goals	0	2

Vialli (27), Di Matteo (59)

Assist
Vialli

Sunday 5 October
Anfield
36,647

Liverpool 4 Chelsea 2
THIRD SENDING OFF IN EIGHT GAMES

Knackered! The team travelled straight to Bratislava airport after the European game and flew home, arriving at Gatwick at 2.30am Friday. At lunchtime they were at the Harlington training ground for a warm down, and after training on Saturday they flew up to Liverpool.

Anfield was returning to its glory days atmosphere after several years of flatness following the introduction of seats on the Kop. Once again the whole ground exploded to the first chords of 'You'll Never Walk Alone' on the public address system and gave a spine-tingling rendition as the teams entered the arena.

One League win for Chelsea here since 1936! In no time at all another bad-tempered battle was gobbing venom. So much at stake, so much to play for.

David Elleray was the referee, the man who had broken Chelsea hearts with his extraordinary penalty decision in the 1994 FA Cup Final. He did not make particularly bad decisions here, although one

certainly affected Chelsea. It's just that he lost the plot early on and the whole match descended into personality clashes.

If only some of Chelsea's players could learn to be as cool as their manager.

As expected Lambourde partnered Clarke at the back, and just as he found the pace of the game difficult on his debut in midfield at Old Trafford and picked up an early booking, so he found it here in his first Premiership game in defence. After twenty-five minutes he was sent off.

He had been booked on fourteen minutes for blocking and bringing down Riedle, the striker from Borussia Dortmund, near the halfway line. Riedle was bursting past him and he reacted instinctively. Liverpool surrounded Elleray demanding a red card there and then.

In the eleven minutes to his red card both sides had scored amid more furious argument and Wise had been booked for an

Zola rounds James to score Chelsea's equalizer

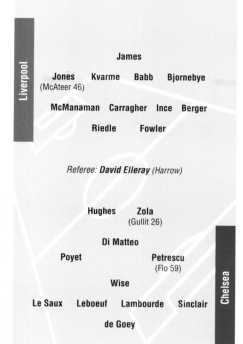

Liverpool

James

Jones (McAteer 46)   Kvarme   Babb   Bjornebye

McManaman   Carragher   Ince   Berger

Riedle   Fowler

*Referee: **David Elleray** (Harrow)*

Hughes   Zola (Gullit 26)

Di Matteo

Poyet   Petrescu (Flo 59)

Wise

Le Saux   Leboeuf   Lambourde   Sinclair

de Goey

Chelsea

aggressive tackle on Fowler.

Liverpool took the lead when a wicked bounce from Ince's long ball evaded Le Saux as he won a race with Berger to the edge of the penalty area, and the Czech Republic international was left to lob the stranded de Goey.

Chelsea equalized two minutes later when Hughes used his bulk to haul Kvarme out of the way of Poyet's pass forward, leaving Zola to race through, round James and score his first away goal of the season.

Liverpool surrounded Elleray, again claiming a foul. And they did so once more when Lambourde felled McManaman as the England international burst past him deep in Chelsea's half. First the yellow card, then the red. Lambourde had been caught out by the pace, but he could have no complaints.

Gullit took off a striker and played 4–4–1. Zola was sacrificed, and on came Gullit himself to play in a flat back four for the first time in his career.

Sadly, the pace of the game caught him out too. No longer was he sweeper, as in his two previous seasons for Chelsea, now he had to mark closely. He wasn't covering, he was stopping. And really, he wasn't fit.

Gullit had become very much a manager who trained when he could. He was nowhere near Premiership fitness. He was looking to get by on knowhow, personality and immense physical presence.

But Chelsea were all over the place, especially down the right-hand side where Petrescu was having problems tracking back.

Berger raced from the centre circle, leaving Di Matteo behind him, to finish from Bjornebye's cross as Chelsea's right-hand side caved in. Liverpool were back in the lead.

Then came that Elleray decision, refusing Poyet a penalty. 'I think Chelsea should have been given a penalty for the foul on Poyet,' admitted Liverpool manager Roy Evans afterwards.

But maybe that would just have papered over the gaps. At half-time Wise needed a painkilling injection after stubbing his toe. What appeared to be a minor aggravation was going to develop into a long-term injury which would cut into the captain's season.

Fowler missed the chance to extend Liverpool's lead before Berger completed his first hat-trick for the Reds, McManaman's long ball charging over Clarke's head with the back four unsure whether they were playing offside or not. Berger rounded de Goey in infuriating style.

Fowler made it four when Berger pulled one back from the left after Chelsea's right-hand side had again been cut open.

The appearance of Flo and a shift to 4-3-2 enhanced Chelsea's performance, and after the Norwegian was denied another clear penalty by Elleray, Chelsea finally got one when McAteer brought Flo down and became the sixth booking of the match. Poyet slotted home.

Gullit's lack of sharpness had been underlined minutes before when he went on an upfield sortie and Wise fed him beautifully, but as he went to round James he slipped and didn't even touch the ball. A literal falling from grace.

Yet his superstar aura was also underlined. 'Ruudi, Ruudi, what's the score?' sang the Kop. He was defending the goal in front of them with his back to them. Play was going on. He turned round, clearly gestured and said: 'Who? Me?', then carried on with his job. The Liverpool supporters roared their approval of him.

	Liverpool	Chelsea
Shots on target	6	2
Corners	3	2
Fouls	15	13
Offsides	8	6
Bookings	2	2

Ince dissent (21), McAteer on Flo (84); Wise, foul (23), Petrescu, foul (41).

Sending off	1	0

Lambourde, two bookings, fouls (14) and (25)

> **We killed ourselves by losing Bernard. That was the key point in the game. They created a lot of chances.**
>
> Ed de Goey

	Liverpool	Chelsea
Goals	4	2

Berger (19, 34, 56), Fowler (63); Zola (21), Poyet (pen) (84)

Assists
Hughes, Flo

Wednesday 15 October
Stamford Bridge
18,671

Chelsea 1 Blackburn Rovers 1

CHELSEA WON 4-1 ON PENALTIES

No place in Europe for the Coca-Cola Cup winners for the first time in nearly thirty years. At least that is what was believed at the time. So Chelsea gave this match low priority and, in truth, winning was not the first aim.

But the game came at a good time. A ten day break for internationals had passed since the Liverpool match, and there were people in need of a game. The big negative factor was the sending off of Vialli.

Two notable forced absentees were the beginning of long-term problems, though only one of them was admitted publicly to be injured at the time. That was Poyet. The man who in twelve games had made such a deep and warm impression on the supporters had collapsed in agony in training on the Saturday when his studs caught in the ground, and the day before had undergone an operation to repair his cruciate ligament. He was lucky to be back before the end of the season.

It was such a blow. He had accepted his role on the left of midfield rather than through the middle and built up a game where he didn't become too peripheral and always looked a classy act on the ball.

The other injury looked like another regular player being rested. But there was no need to rest Wise with his suspension coming up. Unfortunately his stubbed toe had continued to aggravate him and there was swelling in his ankle too. He hadn't trained since the Liverpool game and there was no point in risking him.

Chelsea gave a first game of the season to Hitchcock in goal, a first start to Gullit and first start ever to Babayaro. Newton returned from a summer knee operation to play his first game after two reserve outings. There would be a couple of interesting substitutions too. Blackburn didn't leave out as many regulars but clearly gave the game low priority as well.

In a well contested but uneventful first-half the only two worthwhile efforts on goal brought outstanding saves from Flowers from his own player. Hendry, racing back, knocked Granville's early cross almost past his brilliantly reacting keeper, and then the same player, in trying to block Di Matteo a minute later, was kept out by more superb reactions when he stabbed back Babayaro's low and

Gullit challenges Dahlin

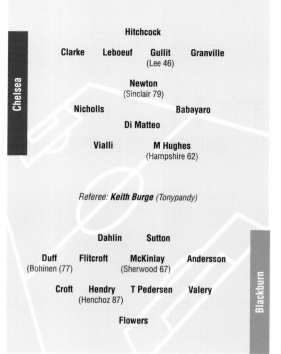

Chelsea

Hitchcock

Clarke   Leboeuf   Gullit   Granville
(Lee 46)

Newton
(Sinclair 79)

Nicholls   Babayaro

Di Matteo

Vialli   M Hughes
(Hampshire 62)

Referee: *Keith Burge* (Tonypandy)

Dahlin   Sutton

Duff   Flitcroft   McKinlay   Andersson
(Bohinen 77)   (Sherwood 67)

Croft   Hendry   T Pedersen   Valery
(Henchoz 87)

Flowers

Blackburn

wicked cross.

Gullit went on a few surges up the right-wing just to give centre-half play a bit of bite, and Chelsea can never have enjoyed two such playmakers in the centre of defence as he and Leboeuf. The surprising thing was they didn't concede a shot on target all half.

Gullit didn't re-appear for the second-half, not as a player anyway, and instead sent on Lee for his first appearance since breaking a leg against Tottenham a year before. As he took his place the crowd gave him a wonderful reception.

But a minute later Blackburn scored. Young Duff got away on the left after Nicholls lost the ball, and Leboeuf's header out fell for McKinlay to launch back a scissors-kick cross shot from just outside the area. Impressive.

Chelsea continued playing good football without setting the world on fire, just little smouldering shocks of smoke here and there.

The equalizer came bang on the hour. It was deserved. Leboeuf accelerated out of defence and his low measured pass split the entire Blackburn team in two. Di Matteo raced away alone and placed the ball out of Flowers' reach. He had scored in every Cup game so far this season.

Gullit immediately sent on youth team striker Steven Hampshire for his debut in place of Hughes. That's how Chelsea were treating the Coca-Cola Cup. Experience before results.

He went on the right flank with Nicholls moving forward. Meanwhile Sutton, bang in form for Blackburn and the country's second top scorer, had only a couple of opportunities, which he wasted.

In extra-time Vialli's skills gave Hampshire his first senior chance which he blasted over from the edge of the area. Then Vialli struck a thirty-yarder which Flowers could only punch away.

Next Valery struck out at Vialli which got the striker angry, and in a case of mistaken identity a few minutes later Vialli struck out at Henchoz. Valery had been booked but Vialli had used his elbow. He became the fourth Chelsea man to be sent off in nine games. Although bookings brought only a Coca-Cola Cup suspension, red cards brought a Premiership suspension. This competition wasn't supposed to result in this sort of problem.

Hampshire pushed forward in the last period to make it 4–3–2. Gullit had learned not to be too defensive when down to ten men. The Blues kept the ball well at the back and the game sailed into a penalty shoot out. In fact substitute Sinclair's explosive sorties forward, outrageous dribbles with wild shots, caused the eleven men of Blackburn several problems and hugely entertained the crowd. Gullit on the bench was laughing with obvious joy.

There was real confidence as the goalkeepers lined up in front of the Matthew Harding Stand. Everyone knew Hitchcock's shoot-out record. And sure enough he dived to his right with an outstretched arm to stupendously block Sutton's first penalty. When Bohinen pathetically chipped over Blackburn's second it was all over. Chelsea had got themselves another game in the tournament.

	Chelsea	Blackburn
Shots on target	2	2
Corners	7	2
Fouls	21	17
Offsides	14	5
Bookings	0	1

Valery on Vialli (101).

Sending off
Vialli, foul (105).

	Chelsea	Blackburn
Penalties	4	1

Leboeuf, Sutton (saved), Sinclair, Bohinen (missed), Clarke, Croft, Nicholls.

' *I think I've only lost two out of about twelve. I had a feeling Sutton was going to go there, I knew he was going to go with pace, so I went full stretch to my right, and it was a comfortable height and another save.* '

Kevin Hitchcock

	Chelsea	Blackburn
Goals	1	1

Di Matteo (60); McKinlay (46)

Assist
Leboeuf

Saturday 18 October
Stamford Bridge
33,365

Chelsea 1 Leicester City 0

SHOTS, SHOTS AND MORE SHOTS

There are two kinds of 1–0 wins that are absolutely brilliant. There's the backs-against-the-wall job, where you either score early and then have to defend for your life with your goalkeeper pulling off world class saves, or else you spend the first eighty-five minutes defending at full stretch and then break out and grab a winner. Then there's the game where you pulverize the opposition with fantastic play but just can't break them down until near the end when you achieve your victory with a top class goal.

This was one of the latter. Leicester, with their strong defence and hard-working midfield, just would not lie down. The goal that finally did for them three minutes from time was one of the best of the season.

Leicester had a French, Guadeloupe-born, twenty-four-year-old debutant in goal. He was a cross between Grobbelaar and Bonetti – lean, incredibly athletic, fantastic hands – a rubber-bodied natural from another age. These days goalkeepers are big and bullying so Pegguy Arphexad should have proved vulnerable. But he didn't.

Chelsea peppered him with goalbound efforts, many from outside the area hit with exquisite power and technique. Eleven were on target, two more hit the woodwork. Corner followed corner.

The well organized, huge and mean Leicester defence headed crosses away, tackled with bludgeoning power on the edge of their box, proved surprisingly mobile when turned, and looked accustomed to standing in tidal waves without toppling.

Now that Gullit had Le Saux and Babayaro available, he decided to try Le Saux in midfield in place of Poyet. It didn't really work.

Di Matteo set the tone with a twenty-yarder which Arphexad seemed to turn over with excessive drama.

Then for ten minutes, before he was called into action again, de Goey had to prove his value with an equally over-the-top diving catch from Claridge's close range header and a superb one-on-one diving save from Heskey.

Three minutes before the half hour Le Saux slipped while attacking the Leicester penalty area and dislocated his elbow. He was in horrible agony. Slowly he was helped from the pitch by physio Mike Banks, all the time holding his arm in place. The Leicester fans gave him a sympathetic reception. It looked like a six week absence for him.

Gullit brought himself on next to Leboeuf with Clarke switching to left-back and Babayaro to the left-wing. Chelsea's passing from the back became sublime as Gullit and Leboeuf constantly broke Leicester in two.

Zola's corner on thirty minutes was missed by Arphexad but Leboeuf headed wide of the target. A minute later Zola got away

Frank Leboeuf celebrates in his own style

Chelsea

de Goey

Sinclair   Leboeuf   Clarke   Babayaro

Newton

Petrescu   Le Saux
(Gullit 28)

Di Matteo
(M Hughes 73)

Flo   Zola
(Vialli 80)

*Referee: **Uriah Rennie** (Sheffield)*

Heskey   Claridge
(Fenton 87)

Guppy   Izzet   Lennon   Campbell   Savage
(Watts 80)

Elliott   Kaamark   Prior

Arphexad

Leicester

after a one-two with Flo but shot wide under pressure from Elliott.

Six minutes before half-time Babayaro turned Prior inside out, twisting and turning as he recovered a cross from the right, and then suddenly unleashed a rising angled drive that nearly took the goal out of the ground. It hit the bar and bounced back into play.

Leboeuf struck a forty-yard thunderbolt which Arphexad turned over. Gullit, stopping, starting, mesmerising, beating his man, started a move carried through by Clarke and Sinclair which finished with Zola shooting from the angle. Arphexad dived and held. Half-time.

Seven first-half corners were followed by ten in the second. Attack, attack, attack.

Zola's brilliant left-wing cross saw Babayaro and Flo getting in each other's way before the latter stabbed a shot straight at Arphexad. Now Chelsea were lining up to shoot. Arphexad saved bravely at Petrescu's feet after another Zola pass; Flo headed wide from Petrescu's cross; and then Flo just failed to reach Sinclair's terrific cross. Three quarters of the game gone.

Graham Rix sent on Hughes for Di Matteo, hoping the extra attacker would win the game.

Gullit fired in a thirty-five-yarder which Arphexad stretched to tip over. Then the goalkeeper blocked at Hughes' feet. Next he produced a brilliant tip-over from another long-range Leboeuf effort. Time was running out.

Finally, after eighty-seven minutes and from Chelsea's fifteenth corner, substitute Vialli laid the ball back

to Leboeuf who again shot from thirty-five yards. The ball lasered into the top corner, and not even Arphexad's outrageous leap across the goal could get anywhere near it. Everyone went mad. What was nearing a disastrous draw was now a victory of the highest drama.

But de Goey was immediately called back to action, palming away Elliott's thirty-yarder at full stretch. Defenders were ruling the day.

Chelsea were now up to fourth with a game in hand over the teams above. What a year.

The winning goal

> **I came with a bottle of champagne for the young Leicester goalkeeper. He'd only played one reserve game, this was his debut, and it was like the Alamo or Custer's last stand. I thought he was magnificent.**
>
> Ken Bates

	Chelsea	Leicester
Shots on target	11	3
Woodwork	2	0
Corners	17	3
Fouls	12	9
Offsides	3	4
Bookings	2	1

Sinclair, foul (77), Babayaro, foul (89); Izzet, dissent (66).

	Chelsea	Leicester
Goal	1	0

Leboeuf (87)

Thursday 23 October
Alfhein Stadium
6,438

Tromsø 3 Chelsea 2

FARCE WITHOUT LAUGHS IN THE SNOW

For the last hour as the plane flew towards Tromsø all you could see was snow. We descended towards the most northern town Chelsea had ever competed in, and towards probably the most northern professional football club anywhere in the world, 210 miles inside the Arctic Circle.

When the wheels bounced comfortably and safely onto the runway a burst of applause broke out from many of the travellers. Relief! The bad flyers aboard were suffering. Fortunately none of the players were particularly bothered.

The airport steward who brought the steps to the door had huge white snowflakes nestling in his full grey beard. Welcome to the old world.

London – and Chelsea – may be cool. Tromsø was bloody freezing.

There was no point in going to the hotel. Who could say if there was going to be a game tomorrow, and there was definitely no chance of training in the stadium.

The travelling party went straight to the ground. The coach carrying the media got stuck for fifteen minutes in the snow.

The Norwegian hosts were charming. Their functional bar overlooked the pitch. These were Vauxhall Conference facilities. The pitch was covered but the Norwegians insisted it would be fit for action. They were dismissive of the masses of heaped snow. The terraces were unrecognizable under snow. No English club would get a safety certificate with this.

Outside the ground cars were literally buried. A park pitch at the back of the ground had mounds of snow behind the goal which were almost as high as the crossbar.

Chelsea trained indoors in a sports centre where out-of-form Tromsø, now at the end of their season, were to play a relegation play-off game on the Sunday. But UEFA wouldn't allow for these facilities to be used for their game. And they were determined the match was to take place. After all, if it was postponed, when could it be played? The snow was set for winter.

So who was going to fancy this match? The team trained again in the sports centre in the morning. Snow was fitful, but surely the kick-off couldn't be guaranteed.

The pitch cover was removed and underneath was a saucepan of spinach. Wet, muddy, uneven, suitable for one thing only, a battle. Kick-off, extraordinarily, was not until 8.45pm. At 8.00pm, after a fair bit of prevarication, the referee pronounced the game on.

Wise had only trained twice since the Liverpool game but he played. Granville came in for Le Saux with Babayaro pushing into midfield. The European pairing of Vialli and Zola were matched up front. Unbelievably, four Chelsea players chose to wear short sleeves. Vialli was one. 'That was the wrong decision. At half-time we were freezing, and in the second-half I wore a shirt with long sleeves and gloves as well, and I felt much better,' he commented afterwards.

Zola the Snowman

Tromsø

Grenersen

SM Johansen   Nilsen   Hansen   Kræmer

Bernsten   B Johansen   Christensen   Fermann
(Hafstad 64)   (Balling 68)

Årst   Lange

Referee: Jacek Granat (Poland)

Vialli   Zola

Babayaro   Wise   Newton   Di Matteo

Granville   Clarke   Leboeuf   Sinclair
(M Hughes 46)   (Myers 86)

de Goey

Chelsea

Chelsea were shambolic. Cumbersome centre-forward Årst should have scored after four minutes when he found himself clear on de Goey and the goalkeeper did well to grab the ball at the second attempt. But a minute later de Goey was nowhere when Di Matteo needlessly conceded a free-kick out wide and Nilsen met Christensen's quick square pass with a twenty-five-yard shot into the corner.

Chelsea tried to keep playing at their own pace and assert their quality but they were swept aside. In the nineteenth minute Christensen burst through the middle and all cover fell apart. Fermann had to chase Lange's pass wide and the danger seemed over, but his acute angled shot bounced in off de Goey's shoulder.

Just before half-time a long high ball into the Chelsea goalmouth found Lange all alone fifteen yards out. He shot wide with de Goey stranded. Would Chelsea have been able to come back from a 3–0 deficit?

As the players left for the interval the blizzard started. In the fifteen minute break the pitch became completely covered, unplayable, dangerous and atrocious. An army of Tromsønions did all they could to clear it. The players came back. Play on!

By now it was unbelievable. The European adventure could be ending in what had started as a farce but was becoming a tragedy. Chelsea needed a goal, so Hughes replaced Granville with Babayaro going to left-back. But Babayaro and too many other Chelsea players wanted to pass the ball. What a joke!

Tromsø had so many chances to go three up. Årst was too slow when Sinclair and de Goey lost their bearings. Lange went round de Goey who was flapping like a walrus, but missed the target. You couldn't play football in this.

The referee stopped play. Surely an abandonment. No – for two minutes the ground staff cleared the lines so they could be seen. Immediately Årst got clear again but chipped wide.

Chelsea's first effort, well wide, came on fifty-nine minutes. Soon after, Zola raced in from an angle and was only just wide. But Tromsø still looked more dangerous. And the blizzard grew worse.

Christensen stung de Goey's palms with a twenty-yarder, Årst had a free header from a long ball into the box, then he beat de Goey to a cross but headed wide. Another two minute break allowed more clearing of lines. Could Europe really be lost like this?

But with five minutes to go Vialli latched on to a long ball, danced to the left of Hansen, tried to poke it through Nilsen to Zola but took advantage of the half-interception to accelerate into the area and score that precious away goal.

Immediately tragedy turned to war. Leboeuf, limping aimlessly, left the field of play, but the UEFA official refused to let Myers replace him. Tromsø kicked off, half of Chelsea weren't even aware they were down to ten men and Årst launched into the hole at the back to make it 3–1. Everywhere there was fury. The whole competition was being undermined.

Then, four minutes later, right on time, brilliance told. Myers' strength and simplicity was better suited to the conditions. He spanked a long ball forward, Hughes headed it down and Vialli slipped past one of the countless Johansens (there were two non-playing substitutes) and coolly scored with his left foot.

If you hadn't known before why Vialli had won so many medals, you did now. But the whole affair was still unforgivable.

	Tromsø	Chelsea
Shots on target	7	2
Corners	4	4
Fouls	21	22
Offsides	4	10
Bookings	1	0
Kræmer on Wise (20).		

> ' The wind was against us, so you look into the snow. It was really ridiculous. I told them just lump it and see where the ball lands. You can't play, you can't dribble, just lump it there and fight. And then the class of Luca made the difference. '
>
> **Ruud Gullit**

	Tromsø	Chelsea
Goals	3	2
Nilsen (5), Fermann (18), Årst (86);		
Vialli (85, 90)		

Sunday 26 October
Reebok Stadium
24,080

Bolton Wanderers 1 Chelsea 0
DEFEAT WITHOUT SOUL, AND FOURTH OF THE SEASON

Whatever the stupidity of playing in those Tromsø conditions, the small town was truly beautiful and the people warm and generous. In that respect it was a delight to be there. Bolton was horrible. Not the people, but the environment. And it wasn't a reaction to tiredness. The team stayed in Tromsø overnight on Thursday. They were delayed leaving in the morning but arrived back at Heathrow at 2.30pm. Di Matteo and Zola flew off to Italy that evening for their World Cup play-off qualifier and were missing on the Sunday. The rest of the squad flew to Manchester on the Saturday.

For the travelling fan the drive from London ended with a traffic jam off the motorway all the way to the stadium car park. No character, no atmosphere, no special local environment. At least Bolton's ramshackle old ground of the last century, Burnden Park, had its pie shops, its meeting places and its local paper at the local newsagent. The Reebok Stadium had access and egress. In and out. No more.

If everywhere were like this we might as well move all the clubs south of Watford and not suffer the tiresome travel. Tromsø – never change.

Long-term injuries were Poyet, Le Saux and Duberry. Suspensions were Wise, Vialli and Lambourde. Bolton were relegation material. Championship competing teams, whatever their problems, should win here. Chelsea didn't.

Petrescu chips over

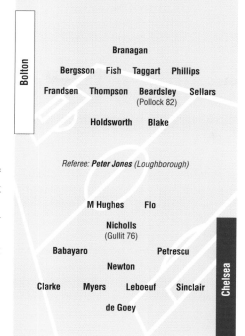

Bolton

Branagan

Bergsson Fish Taggart Phillips

Frandsen Thompson Beardsley Sellars
(Pollock 82)

Holdsworth Blake

Referee: Peter Jones (Loughborough)

Chelsea

M Hughes Flo

Nicholls
(Gullit 76)

Babayaro Petrescu

Newton

Clarke Myers Leboeuf Sinclair

de Goey

Yet it wasn't for the lack of opportunity. Clarke had to play left-back where he was poor going forward. Babayaro in midfield rarely moved after playing the ball and looked far more comfortable in defence. Nicholls kept things ticking over but couldn't penetrate like Di Matteo. Newton was struggling for match fitness and lacked the vision of Wise.

But none of these problems stopped Chelsea totally dominating and creating chance after chance. The style of the season on a good surface, pass and fly, was still well enough oiled to dismiss Bolton easily. Too easily.

Petrescu was given the freedom of the right flank. Has anyone got a better touch or a quicker eye for creating an opening? He did that sublimely. But he was more guilty than anyone of missing chances.

As with Chelsea all season it was a full house. Everyone wanted to see cosmopolitan cool. And this home crowd was silenced by Chelsea's superiority.

Flo raced passed Taggart at will, and an early trip earned the defender a booking. Petrescu took Babayaro's crossfield ball superbly on his chest, tip-toed round Phillips and crossed into an empty box. Leboeuf finished a forty-yard burst with a long-range effort that had Branagan scrambling. Flo went past two in the box from Petrescu's pass and laid back to Hughes, but Branagan smothered the shot. Branagan had an easy diving save when Nicholls failed to score his first League goal, sidefooting tamely on the run. Half-time approached.

Hughes arrived to a lay-back from Petrescu's fierce cross but his ferocious drive was brilliantly turned round. Then a marvellous move between Flo, Nicholls and Hughes finished with Petrescu, perfectly placed, shooting weakly and allowing Branagan to save.

What do you say at half-time? Stop trying to walk the ball into the back of the net. Just get out there and score, score, score!

Chelsea got out there and attacked. Another away win was available here. Three corners were won in the first four minutes. Pass and fly, space everywhere. Nine minutes into the second-half Petrescu broke away for what looked like a certain end to the deadlock but chipped over. A minute later Hughes shot over after Branagan, stretched, had punched Petrescu's cross off Flo's head.

And that was that. The chances dried up, the passing got looser, Clarke and Babayaro looked increasingly exhausted and lost up the left and Bolton gained in confidence. The tide turned.

Bolton new boy Beardsley blazed over when he should have scored. Chelsea's confidence drained.

After seventy-one minutes Holdsworth scored his first goal for his new club, a messy affair after he had nudged on Branagan's clearance. Clarke and Leboeuf got in each other's way and Sellars crossed for Holdsworth to sidefoot home unmarked.

Bolton had chances to extend their lead. They still looked relegation material but now Chelsea did too.

Gullit made a rare appearance, in attacking midfield this time, and although he lacked pace and sharpness he still had the character for one sublime stoppage time cross. Clarke headed it back for Petrescu whose goalbound shot rebounded away off his own man Hughes. It was the defining moment of the afternoon.

Was it weariness? Was it lack of belief? Was it overconfidence? It was, finally, Chelsea's first scoring blank of the season. The last Premiership side to suffer one.

There was still a traffic jam all the way to the motorway an hour after the game.

> '*Chelsea lost against themselves. It was not an excuse that eight were left out. If you don't score the chances that you have, then it's normal in football that if you get one chance for them then it's in. You throw away good opportunities. It's all about scoring goals. Sometimes it was eight yards they didn't score. It's so sloppy.*'
>
> **Ruud Gullit**

	Bolton	Chelsea
Shots on target	5	7
Corners	2	7
Fouls	21	18
Offsides	8	2
Bookings	1	1

Taggart on Flo(7); Babayaro, dissent (85).

	Bolton	Chelsea
Goals	1	0

Holdsworth (71)

Saturday 1 November
Villa Park
39,372

Aston Villa 0 Chelsea 2

UP TO FOURTH, GAME IN HAND OVER TEAMS ABOVE

The last thing you ever do is write off Mark Hughes. Manchester United let him go in 1995 and here he was at Chelsea, still at the top of his trade, another Cup winner's medal in his cabinet and more medals to come.

People claimed he was a bad sale for United but that was harsh on them, after all they won the League and Cup double the following season. It was a good deal all round. It gave the old warhorse the opportunity to win new fans, win more plaudits and set Chelsea up for silverware for the first time in twenty-six years.

Hughes is an extraordinary specimen. A life in the frontline —

the clashing of elbows, the collisions of heads, the stamping of over the top tackles, the constant infiltration of no-go areas — has left him virtually unmarked.

He has the biggest calves and the biggest thighs imaginable. He has a broad chest but small waist. He isn't muscle bound because he's not particularly fussed about lifting weights. He has never suffered a torn muscle.

Mark Hughes is just naturally brutally strong. And he is blessed with a delicate touch which has made him the premier centre-forward target man of his time. He has never possessed pace, his

Hughes heads his birthday goal, Sinclair is head over heels

Aston Villa

Oakes

Ehiogu   Southgate   Scimeca

Charles   Draper   Grayson   Nelson   Wright
                                      (Taylor 60)

Joachim   Yorke
(Milosevic 60)

Referee: Steve Dunn (Bristol)

Chelsea

M Hughes   Zola
                          (Flo 69)

Nicholls   Morris   Newton   Petrescu
           (Di Matteo 63)   (Clarke 69)

Babayaro   Myers   Leboeuf   Sinclair

de Goey

game has always been about pushing to the front, controlling the ball, holding off defenders, and bringing other people into play. So a largely injury-free career was bound to mean a long one because strength and touch generally last longer than pace.

The previous season he was Chelsea Player of the Year and third behind Gianfranco Zola in the national Footballer of the Year poll. Off the pitch he is quiet and unassuming. He changes quickly after training and hurries to Heathrow to fly home to his family in Manchester where they live ten minutes from the airport. In the morning he flies back again.

This was his thirty-fourth birthday. 'It's unfortunate it's fallen on the day of a match otherwise no-one would have noticed how old I'm getting,' he lamented.

After thirty-seven minutes Petrescu's lobbed cross following a short corner was met by Hughes, and his header down at the near post gave Chelsea an interval lead.

Villa, like Bolton the week before, were poor. They were having a poor season and were never going to take advantage of a depleted Chelsea. Wise and Vialli were still suspended. Di Matteo had played for Italy in more snow and even colder conditions than Tromsø in Moscow on Wednesday. Zola had been a non-playing substitute in that game, and the two had only returned to London on the Thursday afternoon. The left side of the team was sorted out with Babayaro retreating to left-back, Clarke dropping to the substitutes' bench, and Morris surprisingly called back in midfield.

Chelsea offered Villa the chance to take the lead. Myers needlessly tripped the twisting Yorke midway through the first half, but Yorke blasted wide from the penalty spot.

Villa were enjoying their largest home crowd of the season to date, but neither side was offering the penetration or sharpness to provide excitement. Chelsea gained the edge when Di Matteo replaced Morris after sixty-three minutes. Di Matteo's ability to glide past opposition and find space opened play up for Chelsea.

At the same time de Goey had to pull off one of his best saves of the season, stretching to turn aside Draper's swerving twenty-five-yard volley.

The three substitutes wrapped the game up. Di Matteo beat his man and fed Hughes out wide, and his lay-back was whipped ferociously and early by Clarke, on in an unaccustomed midfield role, to Flo who at last headed in his second goal of the season. Flo had only replaced Zola three minutes before, the same time as elapsed before his debut goal at Coventry.

De Goey had another save to make from Milosevic's twenty-yarder, but Chelsea and Hughes had a fourth away League win and an eighth clean sheet in seventeen games. If they won the game in hand they would be second. No wonder it was always a full house.

> *It was a good day all round, one of the better birthdays I've had. I had a nice surprise in the morning, I was given the captain's armband, I scored a goal, it was going quite well for me until I got a bump on the head which needed two stitches.*
>
> **Mark Hughes**

> *By their own admission I think they'd say they weren't at their best for the first half hour or so. But that's the sign of a good side: they got their goal and they've really cruised to victory from thereon in.*
>
> **Villa manager Brian Little**

	Aston Villa	Chelsea
Shots on target	2	3
Corners	8	4
Fouls	13	12
Offsides	3	9
Bookings	1	0
Milosevic, dissent (69).		

	Aston Villa	Chelsea
Goals	0	2
M Hughes (37), Flo (82)		
Assists		
Petrescu, Di Matteo, Clarke		
Penalty conceded		
Myers		

Thursday 6 November
Stamford Bridge
29,363

Chelsea 7 Tromsø 1

CHELSEA WON 9–4 ON AGGREGATE

Chelsea's players were surprisingly irate about the first leg in Tromsø. They thought the conditions were a disgrace and the sole reason for their performance. They believed that their sloppiness was only because of the conditions.

They didn't rate Tromsø. They couldn't believe they had lost. The weekend before the first leg Tromsø had lost 4–0 to relegated Lyn Oslo, the defeat which had dragged them into the relegation play-off. In between the two European legs the Norwegians had successfully won that, but big gates and passionate crowds were not something they were used to. And their victory in the first leg ensured a big crowd at Stamford Bridge.

Bad luck, Tromsø. In a romp of glorious passing, clinical finishing and zany celebrations, Chelsea chalked up their third-highest European score ever. They only had eight shots on target. Seven resulted in goals and the eighth in a penalty.

Vialli scored his second hat-trick of the season and took his European tally for the campaign to six, the highest in the competition. 'He is doing well also in Premiership games,' said Gullit afterwards. 'He has made himself again a candidate for the national team. It's always nice to have a man of his charisma and experience.'

Tromsø were poor. But Chelsea's continuing ability to find the net and show such collective joy in doing it was again the talking point. They were increasingly the favourites of the nation.

All the same, the spirited Tromsø forced two early corners to keep everyone on their toes. And one of those Johansens got behind the defence and required a great covering tackle by Di Matteo.

Then it came. Almost as quickly as the snow avalanche in Norway, here was the goal avalanche in West London.

Goal 1: Petrescu raced through the middle on to Wise's pinpoint cross from the right and slanted an unchallenged header into the far corner. He picked up some toilet roll which had been thrown on

Vialli heads his hat-trick goal from Wise's cross

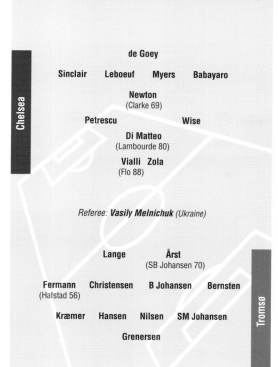

Chelsea

de Goey

Sinclair Leboeuf Myers Babayaro

Newton
(Clarke 69)

Petrescu Wise

Di Matteo
(Lambourde 80)

Vialli Zola
(Flo 88)

*Referee: **Vasily Melnichuk** (Ukraine)*

Lange Årst
(SB Johansen 70)

Fermann Christensen B Johansen Bernsten
(Hafstad 56)

Kræmer Hansen Nilsen SM Johansen

Grenersen

Tromsø

the pitch and offered his boot for his colleagues to clean. This was his first headed goal for Chelsea.

Goal 2: Vialli was clear from Zola's pass after Di Matteo had won the ball in Tromsø's half, and his low early shot caught the goalkeeper unprepared.

Hiccup: The same Johansen who broke clear earlier received Christensen's throw from the left, slipped past Di Matteo and beat de Goey with a low drive from twenty yards. 4-4 on aggregate.

Goal 3: The charging Di Matteo was brought down just outside the penalty area by Hansen who was booked. Zola brilliantly whipped the free-kick into the top corner. Half-time.

Goal 4: Wise's shot was handled by Hansen. Penalty. Hansen dissented and received his second yellow card and was sent off. Leboeuf coolly slotted home the penalty.

Goal 5: Vialli ran in support of Petrescu after the midfielder had burst onto an early pass and dummied magnificently past Kræmer on the halfway line, only to be tackled by the chasing Nilsen just inside the area. Vialli reached the loose ball at an acute angle and slid it in.

Goal 6: Vialli completed his hat-trick with fifteen minutes to go, jumping gloriously to meet Wise's powerful right-wing cross and thumping his header down past the keeper.

Goal 7: Petrescu had just tried to walk the ball round the penalty area and present Vialli with his fourth goal rather than shoot, but had failed. So with five minutes to go he accepted Zola's pass after another fine run, turned his defender and shot smartly home.

In the very last minute Tromsø retrieved some respectability with a thundering twenty-yarder against de Goey's bar. As soon as the whistle blew Vialli marched to the referee and collected the ball. But as he walked off Clarke snatched it from him and rolled it up towards the Matthew Harding Stand so that the hero would have to take his solo acclaim as he fetched it.

Tromsø coach Håkan Sandberg was as polite as the rest of his countrymen throughout the tie. 'Chelsea are one of the favourites to win the competition and in the end they were as good as I knew they were.'

His side were a privilege to face.

> **I'm happy as a baby because I couldn't remember the last time I scored here at Stamford Bridge. I was desperate to score in front of my supporters who have always been great with me, giving me a lot of support, especially when I was down, when I was very sad last season.**
>
> Gianluca Vialli

	Chelsea	Tromsø
Shots on target	8	4
Woodwork	0	1
Corners	5	5
Fouls	6	9
Offsides	15	3
Bookings	0	1
Bernsten on Wise (6)		
Sendings off	0	1
Hansen, foul and dissent (53)		

	Chelsea	Tromsø
Goals	7	1
Petrescu (12, 85), Vialli (23, 60, 75), Zola (42), Leboeuf (pen) (54); B Johansen (38)		
Assists		
Zola 2, Wise 2, Petrescu		

Sunday 9 November
Stamford Bridge
34,382

Chelsea 2 West Ham United 1

FIRST LEAGUE WIN AFTER A EUROPEAN GAME

Ruud Gullit's desire to win took no prisoners. He had shown that in his first season in charge in the away game at Blackburn, Zola's debut and Grodås' League debuts. Having run out of fit sweepers he decided to try Craig Burley there. This was a surprising decision because the year before Glenn Hoddle had given Burley two games at sweeper in the reserves and they had been disastrous. At Blackburn for twelve minutes Chelsea were awful, pinned back without shape, so Gullit abruptly ended his experiment, pushing Burley into midfield. So surprising to the team were his instructions at that early stage that poor Grodås, taking a goal kick while the message was relayed from the touchline, was booked for time wasting.

Gullit's relegation of Vialli to the substitutes' bench for the second half of that season had shown the same attitude to his star signing. All that mattered was winning.

Against Newcastle this season he substituted Paul Hughes after twenty-four minutes. But Hughes was a youngster playing out of position. Against West Ham he substituted one of his star men, Dan Petrescu, after just thirty-four minutes. Petrescu had had a disappointing pre-season when his place seemed to come under threat by Morris, but his early-season form had been outstanding. He had responded well to being pushed forward from wing-back to out-and-out midfielder and had scored plenty of goals.

But the trouble with Chelsea's midfield diamond shape was that if it was not dominating it wasn't always tight enough to battle. That was certainly the case here with Newton still struggling for match fitness, Wise finding two games in four days a struggle for his toe, Di Matteo bombing forward and Petrescu tip-toeing all over the place in the search for penetration. West Ham ruled.

The West Stand lower tier was just about finished and the biggest crowd of the season so far turned out. Nobody expected another Tromsø. Everyone just waited and hoped.

Myers blocked Rowland's cross, Leboeuf escaped what seemed a penalty area trip on Berkovic, Hartson was just wide, another Rowland cross just escaped Lomas after Berkovic had nutmegged Leboeuf, and de Goey saved well from Lomas in a one-on-one.

At the other end a tired Zola mis-hit one shot completely and was beaten by Chelsea old boy Pearce to Hughes' cross after Ferdinand had missed the ball. Yes, Hughes was playing as Gullit continued to ignore reputations. Vialli was on the bench following his hat-trick.

Gullit ditched the midfield diamond, dragged off Petrescu who turned in disbelief and disappeared down the tunnel, sent young Nicholls onto the left flank, pulled Wise into the middle alongside Newton and shifted Di Matteo out to the right. A solid four. It

Zola says 'No' to a big celebration after his cross (see right), leads to an own goal

de Goey

Sinclair Leboeuf Myers Babayaro
(Gullit 90)

Newton

Petrescu Wise
(Nicholls 34)

Di Matteo

M Hughes Zola

Chelsea

Referee: **Graham Barber** (Pyrford, Surrey)

Hartson

Berkovic

Rowland Moncur Lomas Lampard Impey
(Abou 67)

Unsworth Ferdinand Pearce
(Potts 46)

Forrest

West Ham

worked immediately. Wise got into the swing of things and started running the show. Berkovic and Moncur got so upset they had a punch-up between themselves. Zola and Di Matteo had shots requiring saves, and Zola's free-kick right on half-time was headed off the line by Ferdinand.

Wise explained developments. 'We looked very shaky. We did okay but it takes a lot out of you when you keep playing midweek games all the time. I think Dan was very disappointed but the good thing about it is he's taken it and got on with it. That's the way it goes sometimes. Ruudi wanted us going wide and we weren't quite going wide, we were half there and not there, and we seemed to be short in the middle because Roberto was making runs and so was Dan. He wanted to make it more solid with two players holding.'

All the rhythm came flooding back for the second-half and eleven minutes into it Di Matteo took Leboeuf's fine pass up the right and sent Zola away. Zola had lost Ferdinand with his run and his wicked cross deflected off the struggling defender, trying to cover in the goalmouth, and into the net. Chelsea were ahead.

Now Chelsea had total control. Wise's shot was blocked by, of all people, Di Matteo, and Zola's was turned round by Forrest. Sweet passing by Zola and Wise set up Di Matteo who placed his left footer against the post. West Ham started picking up bookings as they clung on, including Pearce on the edge of his own area for bringing down Hughes.

For the second game running Zola

placed the ball and whipped the free-kick into the top corner. Oh happy day.

But, of course, Chelsea life is not that simple. Almost immediately Myers fouled West Ham's new forward, substitute Abou, when he was caught out trying to dribble away from him in the penalty area. Hartson drilled in the low spot-kick.

And right on time Berkovic raced through the middle only to be tripped by Leboeuf on the edge of the area. Leboeuf lay in a heap and was booked. Gullit took no chances. He substituted him with himself to ensure that Chelsea would defend the free-kick with eleven men. And that was that. Job done, resolution discovered when required and flair ignited for long enough to win. The three points took Chelsea up to fourth, three points behind the leaders with a game in hand.

Next day Wise was back in treatment for his toe. And two days later Petrescu was fine. He hadn't been spoken to by Gullit, nor had he approached him. 'English players are different. In Italy, in Romania also, you never go to the manager and say, "Why did you do that?" He is the manager and so you accept his decisions.'

	Chelsea	West Ham
Shots on target	9	3
Woodwork	1	0
Corners	9	5
Fouls	15	12
Offsides	1	2
Bookings	2	3

Hughes, foul (78); Leboeuf,foul (90); Rowland on Hughes (76); Pearce on Hughes (81), Abou on Babayaro (90).

❝*We know now that all the teams that come here to play against us are afraid of us and they play a defensive game. We have to work out how to score a goal. So far we did that and we are satisfied. Today was in a better position for me [than on Wednesday against Tromsø when he also scored from a free-kick], but when they go in they are all good. The first one was good as well [Ferdinand headed off the line] but it was a little bit low, so I just made sure it was a little bit higher.*❞

Gianfranco Zola

	Chelsea	West Ham
Goals	2	1

Ferdinand (og) (56), Zola (82); Hartson (pen) (86)

Assist
Zola

Wednesday 19 November
Stamford Bridge
20,968

Chelsea 2 Southampton 1
AFTER EXTRA TIME, 1—1 AFTER NINETY MINUTES

What an enjoyable evening. There was still no European qualification expected for the Coca-Cola Cup winners, so once again Ruud Gullit used the full range of his squad. Southampton, who had won five of their last six games, played their first team.

Southampton manager Dave Jones accepted defeat by Chelsea Reserves gracefully – well, almost Reserves. 'Ruud was a bit unfortunate. He was down to his last eighteen pros,' he commented.

In an open game of defensive frailties and attacking attempts to impress, Chelsea smacked in the most shots on target all season, conceded most too, and won most corners. Surprisingly it was all the more delightful because it didn't seem to matter, due to the European thing, and because it was 'our boys' against 'their men'.

Principal boy was Nick Crittenden. In his first year as a professional following two years on a youth training scheme, he had played almost solely at wing-back. Now on his first team debut he had to operate in a midfield four and he gave Benali a torrid time. 'He was for me the best player on the pitch,' said Gullit, 'playing with flair. He was going forward, good crosses, tried to hit balls long distance.'

The man who struggled most was Gullit himself. A few right-wing forays aside, interesting diversions for a centre-half, he clearly fought against lack of fitness. The day before his girlfriend had given birth to a daughter and his distractions were added to by the start of a coaching course in Holland on Mondays which was to last the season.

In the first five minutes Hirst blasted over from eight yards and Morris brought an exceptional save from Jones with a twenty-yard strike. Morris struck again from twenty-five yards on the half-hour,

Babayaro hugs Morris after the youngster had driven home his late winner

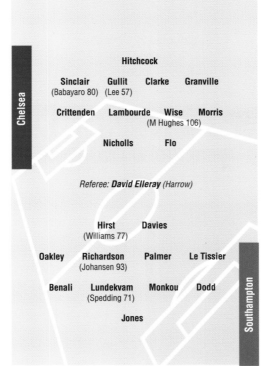

Chelsea

Hitchcock

Sinclair (Babayaro 80) Gullit (Lee 57) Clarke Granville

Crittenden Lambourde Wise Morris (M Hughes 106)

Nicholls Flo

*Referee: **David Elleray** (Harrow)*

Hirst (Williams 77) Davies

Oakley Richardson (Johansen 93) Palmer Le Tissier

Benali Lundekvam (Spedding 71) Monkou Dodd

Jones

Southampton

forcing another save, and Hitchcock did his bit by smothering Hirst's close-range effort.

Once again the Coca-Cola Cup was proving of use to Gullit. Wise, still not training properly, needed match practice. Di Matteo and Zola, away on international duty the weekend before, could be rested, giving the likes of Nicholls and Morris rare starts and Flo a home game.

Early in the second-half Davies, the strong and impressive young Southampton striker, got away from Gullit and the defence three times. On the first Clarke intervened, on the second Hitchcock blocked but on the third he chipped the ball over the advancing goalkeeper to give Southampton the lead.

Chelsea ploughed forward without care. Sinclair had a header cleared off the line, and within ten minutes Chelsea were level. Flo ran onto Crittenden's pass down the right touchline to get behind Benali, swung inside Lundekvam, and running square along the eighteen-yard line crashed a low left-footer past Jones. What a great goal for your first home strike!

Chelsea won thirteen corners in the extraordinary second-half as the game pinballed from end to end. Nicholls, desperate for his first senior goal, was twice foiled by Jones, and so was Wise after cutting inside Monkou. Hitchcock had to be athletic to palm away Palmer's forty-five-yarder after a mis-hit clearance. Flo's effort was deflected and Davies shot narrowly wide.

More goals had to come. But they didn't, Hitchcock rescued the situation after getting in a mix-up with substitute Babayaro, somehow turning round Le Tissier's mis-hit shot with five minutes

left. Granville cleared off the line after Lee, substitute for Gullit, had half-blocked Davies, and then Nicholls shot straight at defender Benali from six yards out. He covered his face in anguish. After all, he was a full-time striker until nine months ago.

Extra time then. Not what you really want when there is an important and difficult League game at Blackburn on Saturday. The play slowed. But Hitchcock's tip-over from the irrepressible Davies kept him centre stage.

It looked a certain penalty shoot-out again. The match started drifting. Yet with three minutes left Chelsea won it.

Jody Morris hadn't had a good season and he wasn't having a good match. Stuck out on the left of midfield he looked slow, overweight and lacking in sharpness. All the skills he brought to the team as an eighteen year old a year before seemed to have gone. Just those two first-half shots had lit up his performance. Until now.

Lee raced forward from the back, fed Hughes on the edge of the area and kept running. Hughes used that as a decoy and laid the ball back to Morris. The youngster thumped another long distance effort and this one zipped into the corner past a flailing Jones. Morris ran to the Matthew Harding Stand, arms raised, ticket booked for the next round. Chelsea Reserves – almost – 2, Southampton 1. It felt good.

In the minutes remaining the score could have changed. Flo was blocked by Jones, Hitchcock held Palmer's header and right on time Hitchcock made a point-blank save from Le Tissier's header. If you won – and Chelsea had – there were heroes everywhere.

> ' *Graham [Rix] told me on Monday, said I was starting, so I had a couple of days to psych myself up for it, lose all the nerves. As soon as the whistle blew I was all right. Dennis Wise gave me a lot of support, Ruud Gullit, and Steve Clarke probably the most. They kept urging me on.* '
>
> **Nick Crittenden**

	Chelsea	Southampton
Shots on target	14	10
Corners	21	7
Fouls	10	5
Offsides	5	6
Bookings	0	2

Davies on Sinclair (19), Palmer on Wise (62).

Chelsea	Southampton
Goals	2	1

Flo (61), Morris (117); Davies (51)

Assist
M *Hughes*

Saturday 22 November
Ewood Park
27,683

Blackburn Rovers 1 Chelsea 0

ANOTHER DEFEAT BY A TOP FIVE TEAM

Frustration at Ewood

Every season has a game or two where you feel there's a turning point. At the time, I felt this was one. As I drove away from the foul muddy car park across the one-way system from Blackburn's ground, I said to my team of programme and *Onside* contributors: 'That's it, we can't win the League.'

As it turned out, Chelsea could have, and would challenge for a lot longer yet. But Blackburn away crippled the belief in me.

There were a number of factors. Chelsea hadn't beaten Blackburn – the Coca-Cola shoot-out between their half-reserve sides a few weeks before excepting – since 1988. Chelsea had to show improvement. They didn't. Since switching from a 3–5–2 formation to 4–4–2 for the FA Cup semi-final the previous season, Chelsea had failed to beat any of the top five sides. The Chelsea tradition was always to get to the brink of a position of challenging and then to lose. They had to show improvement. They didn't.

The media view that Chelsea were losing too many games had rightly been scorned by the club. Chelsea were winning more than other clubs and two extra points for a game won rather than drawn was better than the one for a draw rather than a defeat. But Chelsea had chances to get a draw at Ewood Park and that, most importantly, would have meant only one point for Blackburn rather than three. As it was, Blackburn moved up to second. It was a game where at least a point was required.

Yes, Chelsea had lost to Arsenal and Liverpool only when down to ten men, but they were down to ten men because they were struggling and committing bookable offences. Although Winterburn for Arsenal and now Croft for Blackburn scored rare and outstanding goals, that can't be an excuse.

Croft's goal after ten minutes was the first significant action of the game. Clarke, back in the centre of defence for the injured Myers, conceded a free-kick to Sutton, and when Babayaro headed out Ripley's cross no-one closed down Croft. He had been at Blackburn for nearly two years without scoring but now he half-volleyed a rising, near-post thunderball in off the underside of the bar.

'The unfortunate thing is all the time we get beaten by somebody who never scores in his whole life and then scores a cracker,' said Gullit. 'Not a silly goal, what can we do about that? The chances we created and the way we played, you wanted to have something more out of the game.'

He was right. Chelsea should have drawn. The chances were there. The chief culprit, of all people, was Zola. His worst miss was a minute before half-time when he jumped to meet Wise's cross and somehow sliced a free header wide from five yards out. A little earlier he had tackled Wise's long pass through Flowers outside the goalkeeper's area, but had been unable to beat Kenna in a race for the ball as it dropped towards the goal.

Then four minutes after half-time Wise headed a Sinclair cross back to him fifteen yards out and in space. Zola dragged his left-foot shot wide.

On the flight home after the game, grief stricken, he approached managing director Colin Hutchinson and said: 'I just want to say, Mr Colin, I am sorry for missing those chances today.'

Just before and after those misses Flowers saved well from Wise and Petrescu, and with Leboeuf defending superbly and passing as well as ever and Wise controlling midfield, it is not surprising that the Chelsea management team and players read less into the defeat than I did in the press box.

But the fact remains that when Gullit sent on Flo for Petrescu with twenty minutes to go Chelsea never looked like scoring. It was de Goey who was twice called into action before the end. Leboeuf limped off with a groin strain with nine minutes to go and Newton left the field with increasing pain in his foot. His injury was the worst. An X-ray later in the week would reveal a stress fracture and the injury-plagued midfielder was set for another six weeks of frustration.

The frustration in me was different. Blackburn were good – methodical and professional – but they weren't that good. Chelsea were brilliant. But they hadn't been brilliant enough.

Zola's finishing touch deserts him

> ‘We played good football. We were unlucky because the man scored a very good goal. We had four great chances but we didn't score. Blackburn play well too and it was a good footballing game. Franco had two great chances and he missed, but you can't say something to Zola because he's scored too many goals very important for us. That's football.’
>
> Frank Leboeuf

	Blackburn	Chelsea
Shots on target	5	3
Corners	6	7
Fouls	21	18
Offsides	6	9
Bookings	1	3

Gallacher on Leboeuf(32); Newton, foul (53), Di Matteo, foul (61), Sinclair, foul (68).

	Blackburn	Chelsea
Goal	1	0
Croft (10)		

Wednesday 26 November
Stamford Bridge
34,148

Chelsea 2 Everton 0
GAME IN HAND OVER LEADERS WON, UP TO THIRD

Chelsea changed its essential character under Ruud Gullit, but no-one outside the club seemed to notice. Chelsea were notorious for losing the games they ought to win and upsetting the glory boys when they were expected to lose. They were almost predictable in their unpredictability.

Now, apart from the occasional lapse which every team suffers, not only were they winning the games they ought to win, they were frequently annihilating the opposition. But when it came to the glory boys, the top teams, they were no longer accruing the points.

Wily old defender Steve Clarke offered an answer. 'It's because we're a top team who the other top teams take seriously. Before, they didn't really take us seriously, they weren't properly up for the game, so we could catch them out. Now, they're desperate to beat us, they prepare properly and play at their best.'

So, after the defeat at Blackburn, here was a real test of the new Chelsea character. Everton were bottom. This was the game the club had held in hand over everyone since the first week of the season when the Shed and West Stand lower tier were being finished. Now we would see for certain where Chelsea stood.

Everton didn't arrive in the best of shape. Manager Howard Kendall looked under pressure. He was giving a debut at right wing-back to Mitch Ward whom he had just signed as part of a swap deal from Sheffield United which involved former Chelsea midfielder Graham Stuart going the other way.

As expected, Gullit was without Leboeuf and Newton. Duberry, however, returned again, recovered from his ankle injury of two months ago. But he hadn't had a reserve game. Wise switched back to the middle and the problem left-of-midfield slot – remember, no Poyet or Le Saux – was taken by Nicholls. The youngster had been impressing more as a substitute than a starter, so here was an important chance for him. Vialli was given his first League start in two months. The crowd greeted his selection with a huge cheer. Top scorer by far, the increasing overlooking of him by Gullit was not being deemed as just as in the previous season. But Gullit was managing Chelsea's best League campaign of the decade, so who could argue.

Everton played five at the back and battled for their life. The game was no better than Saturday's. The full house – the only spare seats were in the Everton section – spurred the team on, but it was hard work.

Zola's recent good run with free-kicks forced Ferguson to withdraw to the goalline for one on the edge of the box, and he headed away when Southall was beaten midway through the first-half. Southall then saved well after Di Matteo had cut inside Short when Nicholls headed on Clarke's long pass. Just before half-time Vialli went round Hinchcliffe after Zola and Wise had combined well, but although his cross-shot beat the goalkeeper it went wide of the far post.

Early on, one towering header by the giant Ferguson aimed at Speed had been crucially cleared by Clarke, and five minutes into the second-half Chelsea survived their closest ordeal. Ferguson rose again and smacked a header from Ward's cross against de Goey's post from twelve yards out.

Problems suddenly unfolded. Clarke stretched his calf and Nicholls stretched his groin. They were replaced by Granville, battling through sinusitis, and Mark Hughes. Hughes joined Vialli up front with Zola switching to the left. It didn't work.

Everton were having a good spell. Wise got booked yet again for

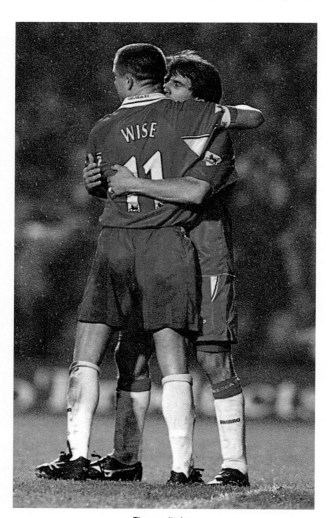

The penalty boys

Duberry clears from Ferguson

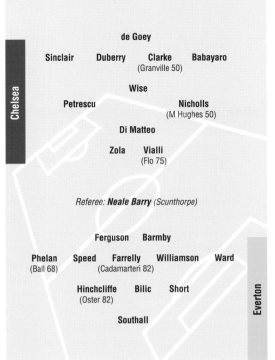

Chelsea

de Goey

Sinclair   Duberry   Clarke   Babayaro
(Granville 50)

Wise

Petrescu   Nicholls
(M Hughes 50)

Di Matteo

Zola   Vialli
(Flo 75)

Referee: **Neale Barry** *(Scunthorpe)*

Ferguson   Barmby

Phelan   Speed   Farrelly   Williamson   Ward
(Ball 68)   (Cadamarteri 82)

Hinchcliffe   Bilic   Short
(Oster 82)

Southall

Everton

tripping Bilic. The supply dried up and although a number of corners were won — the corner count of 10–1 to Chelsea correctly reflected the home team's superiority — you couldn't see a goal coming.

Indeed, when de Goey had to turn over Ferguson's lob with twenty minutes remaining, a breakthrough goal for Everton seemed as possible as one for Chelsea. Di Matteo had switched to the left with Zola at the front of the midfield diamond but the balance still wasn't there. Finally, to the boos of the crowd Gullit took off Vialli in the seventy-sixth minute and brought on Flo. More importantly, he pushed Zola back up front and tried Hughes in midfield.

Hughes excelled. One brutal tackle to win possession in the Everton half was vintage in character, but altered in style from centre-forward play to midfield battler.

Time seemed to be running out. Di Matteo, whose season so far had been erratic but was beginning to blossom, made the breakthrough. He dribbled into the penalty area, got outside Ward and had his legs taken from him. Penalty!

Who would take it? There was no Leboeuf, and no Poyet who scored at Liverpool. Zola scored at Wembley in the Charity Shield shoot-out but had missed pre-season in the Umbro Tournament so Wise took the responsibility. He had not taken a penalty, not even a shoot-out one, since missing at home to Aston Villa the week after the FA Cup semi-final against Manchester United in 1996. He drilled confidently home. Even though Southall dived the right way he had no chance.

Right on time Flo burst onto Sinclair's long ball, and Bilic was sent off for tripping him as he sprinted into the area. This time Wise invited Zola to take the penalty, and he drove into the opposite corner with Southall wrong-footed.

Chelsea hadn't played well, but they had deserved to win. They had now played the same number of games as everyone else and were third, three points behind the leaders, Manchester United. Yet another clean sheet had been collected. Everton manager Kendall told his players not to talk to the media and refused to give a press conference himself. Chelsea players were available to everyone and everyone wanted them.

The different pressures between top and bottom could not have been clearer.

	Chelsea	**Everton**
Shots on target	5	3
Woodwork	0	1
Corners	10	1
Fouls	11	13
Offsides	4	2
Bookings	1	3

Wise, foul (54); Short on Nicholls (32), Hinchcliffe, not withdrawing ten yards (36), Ferguson on Wise (56).

Sending Off	0	1

Bilic, professional foul (90)

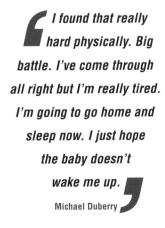

> **I found that really hard physically. Big battle. I've come through all right but I'm really tired. I'm going to go home and sleep now. I just hope the baby doesn't wake me up.**
>
> **Michael Duberry**

	Chelsea	**Everton**
Goals	2	0

Wise (pen) (80), Zola (pen) (90)

Assists
Di Matteo, Flo

Saturday 29 November
Stamford Bridge
34,544

Chelsea 4 Derby County 0
UP TO SECOND

Gianfranco Zola – the Footballer of the Year, the man with happy feet. The most wonderfully gifted footballer, small on physique but a giant in vision. The previous season he had scored a series of fantastic goals. But this season the goals had dried up. Only two before November. And in November, two from free-kicks and one from a penalty. None from open play.

The media started debating his form. Italy had dropped him to the substitutes' bench. Gullit defended him, said he was happy with his performances and that was what was important, but the debate continued.

It was crazy because Chelsea were third, having their best season in years and playing the best football in the country. Zola topped assists with Petrescu and Luca Vialli had only one assist against Franco's seven. Zola's football was telling.

So a lot was going right. But the lack of goals, the debate, and the Italian situation did seem to nibble at his confidence. Italy had played him wide on the left against England where he had been poor. Every game for Chelsea had screamed out that he should be the free man off the front forward, attacking the penalty area with vision. He lacked the pace and strength to attack from elsewhere. If a bloke's got world class ability surely you play round it.

Chelsea played to Zola's world class ability today. Today was glorious. Today Chelsea rose to second place and stuffed sixth-placed Derby with a range of attacking skills that were the peak of

Zola hooks his second goal

was a part of that. It was crazy because Chelsea were the second top scorers in the Premiership and Zola was a forward. Yes, Vialli had scored double the number of goals and looked on fire, but Zola

the season. And they did it in front of their biggest home gate for four years. Gianfranco Zola scored the most wonderful hat-trick you could hope to witness.

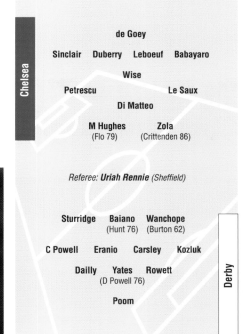

Chelsea

de Goey

Sinclair   Duberry   Leboeuf   Babayaro

Wise

Petrescu   Le Saux

Di Matteo

M Hughes   Zola
(Flo 79)   (Crittenden 86)

*Referee: **Uriah Rennie** (Sheffield)*

Sturridge   Baiano   Wanchope
        (Hunt 76)   (Burton 62)

C Powell   Eranio   Carsley   Kozluk

Dailly   Yates   Rowett
(D Powell 76)

Poom

Derby

If the season had started well, it was now unbelievable. How long could the side ride this wave?

Derby helped. They played a hopelessly attacking 3–4–3 formation and Chelsea destroyed them in midfield. Pass and fly.

'Chelsea were the best team we've come up against this season," said Derby defender Gary Rowett. 'There were times when there were three players running at you and you just didn't know what to do for the best.'

Derby manager Jim Smith made no excuses. 'We did quite well. It could have been eight! We were a bit soft to be fair, men against boys, but I thought Chelsea were outstanding. Zola and Hughes were brilliant. Duberry at the back makes a big difference for them.'

Le Saux returned from six weeks out with a dislocated shoulder and Chelsea had more balance again even though he played in midfield.

Chelsea started off with terrific pace. The first goal after eleven minutes was pure perfection.

De Goey passed out to Babayaro

who pushed the ball on to Le Saux. Le Saux threaded a delightful thirty-five-yard pass along the touchline to Hughes. He shrugged off Rowett, cut into the area and then laid the ball back to Di Matteo. Di Matteo thought about a shot but squared the ball to Zola, unmarked twenty-five yards out. He set the ball up and fired it low into the far corner. Oh happy feet.

The second goal eleven minutes before half-time wasn't in the same class but was fun. A trademark Hughes overhead kick after Yates had sliced his clearance from Le Saux's cross wasn't executed properly, but the ball bounced awkwardly over Poom's dive.

The third goal after sixty-five minutes was working class. Di Matteo dispossessed Eranio in the Derby half, the referee fortunately saying no foul, and sent Hughes away. Poom couldn't hold his powerful shot although he recovered well to block Zola's follow-up. But Poom could only look on as Zola chased the ball across the six-yard box and turned it inside the post.

The fourth goal eleven minutes later was world class. Zola was in the inside-left channel a third of the way inside Derby's half when a pass was drilled to him from the halfway line. It was well inside him when he athletically back-heeled it while in mid-air to Di Matteo and in one movement turned and left his marker for dead. Di Matteo returned the ball perfectly and Zola hared through to place it beyond Poom.

Surprisingly it was his first ever hat-trick. Maybe it's because he creates more goals than he scores. The previous season Chelsea had more scorers than in any other year in their history. This season there would be almost as many. The whole team was outstanding. But Zola was the cream. Lay off Zola!

	Chelsea	Derby
Shots on target	9	2
Woodwork	1	0
Corners	10	1
Fouls	14	9
Offsides	2	4
Bookings	3	3

Sinclair, foul (50), M Hughes, foul (55), Di Matteo, foul (68); Sturridge on Wise (38), Carsley on Wise (54), D Powell on Petrescu (81).

> **The third one maybe was the best, the action was perfect, Robbie's pass was magnificent. I made a good run from behind, I flicked the ball to Robbie with my heel. It was a great day. Really today I think Chelsea played quality football. The game I think must be sent to the schools. I don't want to exaggerate, but it really was quality football.**
>
> Gianfranco Zola

	Chelsea	Derby
Goals	4	0

Zola (11, 65, 76), M Hughes (34)

Assists

M Hughes 2, Di Matteo 3

Saturday 6 December
White Hart Lane
28,476

Tottenham Hotspur 1 Chelsea 6
BIGGEST EVER WIN OVER SPURS

How can you improve on Derby? Easy – play Tottenham! Chelsea were undefeated in seventeen games against their close rivals from North London. Seventeen! Really, it was sixteen, but no Chelsea fan could discount the 4–0 Makita Tournament Final win at White Hart Lane in 1993. Tony Cascarino got a hat-trick that day.

Well, this beat that game and the rest ends up. 'Sing when you're drawing, you only sing when you're drawing,' taunted the Chelsea fans as Tottenham dropped into the relegation zone.

In truth, the team didn't play that well, certainly nowhere near as well as the previous week. Gullit pulled out another astonishing piece of team selection. Hughes was suspended for three games following this one due to his booking against Derby, so on the squad system theory he seemed a certain starter, particularly after his fine display last Saturday. But he was on the bench as Flo made a rare start.

'I put out a team that I thought should win the game,' said Gullit. 'Tore Andre Flo scored three and showed that everyone in the squad wants to play. He is a big lad, but also very agile and technical.'

Flo accepted his place and the fact that he might lose it the following week despite his hat-trick with equanimity. 'I think that training is a qualification for the team as well as the matches. You have to be good in training the day after.'

Missing from the score sheet was Zola. But he could claim a cool four assists. The finishing was remarkable. Every on-target second-half shot for Chelsea was a goal. It was 1–1 at half-time. And without two scintillating de Goey saves when the scores were goalless, who knows what might have happened.

After two minutes his parry from Ginola's fifteen-yard piledriver was unbelievable and before the half hour his top corner tip-over from the same player was equally magnificent. Like Di Matteo, the

Flo scoring the first

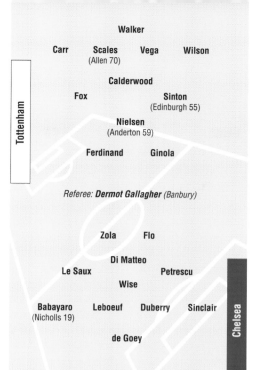

Tottenham

Walker

Carr   Scales   Vega   Wilson
        (Allen 70)

Calderwood

Fox   Sinton
                    (Edinburgh 55)

Nielsen
(Anderton 59)

Ferdinand   Ginola

Referee: Dermot Gallagher (Banbury)

Zola   Flo

Di Matteo

Le Saux   Petrescu

Wise

Babayaro   Leboeuf   Duberry   Sinclair
(Nicholls 19)

de Goey

Chelsea

big goalkeeper was going into top gear for the second half of the season.

In between those two saves Tottenham's Walker made two of his own, tipping round from Petrescu after a typical Chelsea quickly switching the ball move, then keeping out Leboeuf's thirty-five-yarder from the resulting corner.

Struggling Tottenham were battling well in their first home game under new manager Christian Gross. Nielsen was especially aggressive in midfield. Problems built on that left-hand side for Chelsea when Babayaro limped off in the twentieth minute with pain in his troublesome foot. Le Saux dropped to left-back and Nicholls came on. It was going to be a marvellous afternoon for him too.

With six minutes remaining in the first-half the breakthrough came.

Goal 1: Flo rose at the near post to head Zola's super left-sided cross past Walker.

Hiccup: Tottenham equalized four minutes later when Vega rose above Leboeuf to head in a wide free-kick from Sinton which Leboeuf himself had conceded.

Goal 2: Di Matteo bowed on the run into Petrescu's deflected cross from the right after Zola's holding up of play had again been crucial. Di Matteo had now scored in all of his three games against Tottenham.

Goal 3: Tottenham were falling apart. Sinton had limped off and been replaced by Edinburgh with Chelsea old boy Clive Wilson switching to sweeper. Two minutes after the second goal Wilson

had alertly tracked Petrescu's magnificent diagonal run into the box and blocked his attempt to score from Leboeuf's outrageous pass from the centre circle. Now Petrescu and Leboeuf repeated their brilliance and Edinburgh couldn't cope. Petrescu flick-volleyed first time with the outside of his boot over Walker. One of the goals of the season.

Goal 4: Why didn't Tottenham replace Sinton with the not very fit Anderton? Now they used Anderton to replace the strong Nielsen through the middle and Tottenham's midfield collapsed. They were playing 4–4–2 again. Flo played a one-two with Zola, the return lobbing Scales, and he crashed his second past Walker.

Goal 5: At last, at last. Nicholls smacked in his first League goal. Calderwood pathetically missed the ball from a throw-in, Zola raced away and fed Nicholls who cut inside Carr and drove in. 'I was most happy for Mark Nicholls,' said Gullit, despite Flo's hat-trick. 'He has worked so hard and deserves his goal.'

Goal 6: Leboeuf delivered an exquisite outside-of-the-boot chip from the centre circle and Flo was away. Walker left his line and the striker delicately chipped him. Brilliant.

Flo's was Chelsea's fourth hat-trick of the season, the first time the team had achieved that many since 1984/85. He was the third player to score one, the first time that had happened since 1968/69.

It felt like the goals would never dry up.

	Tottenham	Chelsea
Shots on target	7	9
Corners	4	5
Fouls	8	10
Offsides	5	0
Bookings	0	1
Di Matteo, foul (51).		

> *Ed was outstanding today, he saved two outstanding shots from Ginola, and two or three shots in the second-half. We have to thank him today, we needed him a lot.*
>
> Frank Leboeuf

	Tottenham	Chelsea
Goals	1	6
Vega (43); Flo (39, 62, 89), Di Matteo 47, Petrescu (59), Nicholls (77)		
Assists		
Zola 4, Petrescu, Leboeuf 2		

Saturday 13 December
Stamford Bridge
34,690

Chelsea 0 Leeds United 0

NINE MEN LEEDS SHUT OUT CHELSEA

Blackburn away, Leeds at home. Every season has a game or two where you feel there's a turning point. Just when it seems there's no way the goals can dry up, they dry up. Leeds had two players sent off in the first-half but Chelsea barely troubled goalkeeper Martyn all game.

Leeds were tough. Chelsea had a reputation for wilting in the force of such sides. Leeds were fifth. Chelsea couldn't budge them.

For forty-five minutes in the second half Leeds played 4–3–1 as Chelsea attacked the Matthew Harding Stand end. Even Leeds' one front man was mostly behind the ball. They defended with passion and unity. For relief they hacked the ball away and didn't chase it, simply re-forming for the next assault.

Chelsea, by contrast, quickly lost shape. All that one-touch, switch-and-move, pass-and-fly, flick-and-shoot brilliance on the edge of the penalty area that had destroyed teams all season suddenly died. Why?

Hughes was suspended. Radebe started by man-marking Zola and marked him so badly after five minutes with a disgraceful scything from behind that he was booked. It was Leeds' second booking. Zola fought well in the first-half but when he was no longer man-marked in the second surprisingly got lost in the mess. Flo, so frequently impressive as a substitute, and lately also as a starter, was equally anonymous.

In midfield the increasing problem of Dennis Wise was being sorted out. He was losing that extra sharpness of earlier in the season. He had barely trained now for over two months. The toe and related ankle problem was getting no better. Perhaps he could train the day before a game, but anything else would exacerbate the swelling too much. He could run. General fitness wasn't a problem. Playing football was the problem.

On the Thursday he'd gone for a scan which again showed no hidden hairline fractures or other untreated damage. Somehow, after that stubbed toe at Liverpool, he had developed a tissue disorder which would only go in its own time and with rest. He was swallowing anti-inflammatory pills and antibiotics every day in a battle against it. But it wouldn't budge.

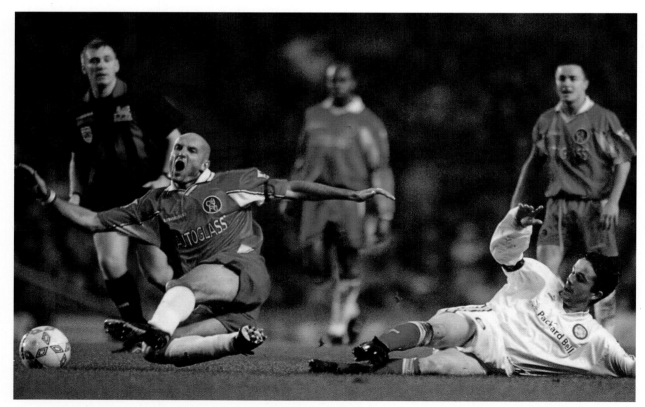

Kelly fouls Leboeuf

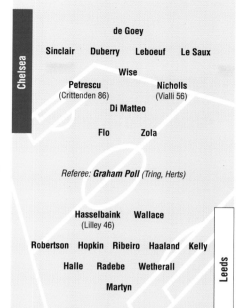

Chelsea

de Goey

Sinclair Duberry Leboeuf Le Saux

Wise

Petrescu   Nicholls
(Crittenden 86)   (Vialli 56)

Di Matteo

Flo Zola

*Referee: **Graham Poll** (Tring, Herts)*

Hasselbaink Wallace
(Lilley 46)

Robertson Hopkin Ribeiro Haaland Kelly

Halle Radebe Wetherall

Martyn

Leeds

So it was agreed that the physio staff would prepare him for every game and there would no longer be pressure on him to train. His passing, his captaincy, his knowhow and his competitiveness all seemed so crucial to the side.

Against Leeds, surprise, surprise, he was booked. He just couldn't stay out of the trouble. He was booked after a tangle with Haaland after twenty-four minutes; it was Chelsea's second booking. Haaland immediately attacked him and became Leeds' fourth booking. Unfortunately for Haaland he'd also been their third and was sent off.

The first-half saw Leeds being thuggish, dirty and stupid. 'I don't know why we started like that,' said their manager George Graham. 'Maybe it was because they thought they were going to be playing one of the title challengers, a very talented team.'

Wise's booking was stupid as well. It brought his second suspension and would cover the third round FA Cup tie, just drawn, at home to Manchester United.

Elsewhere in midfield there were problems. Nicholls, like Flo, had done better as a substitute than when starting. Two of Poyet, Babayaro and Le Saux on the left always seemed to be injured. On the right Petrescu wanted to pass and move and turn up all over the pitch come what may. But he provided no natural width. With nine Leeds defenders to get past, Chelsea needed width yet kept trying to play through the middle. Petrescu found himself substituted by the novice Crittenden near the end.

Chelsea struggled. Crowd anger at the disgraceful Leeds performance kept the support fully behind the home team. The worst foul of the first half, Ribeiro on Wise, didn't even get a caution, but after their fifteen fouls before half-time they had seven bookings, and Kelly was sent off right on the interval for his second cautionable offence. A win and retention of second place seemed inevitable.

The first shot on target did not arrive until fifty-four minutes. Martyn easily collected from Flo. A series of crossfield balls were too predictable to outmanoeuvre Leeds. The lack of attacking set play practice beyond Zola's shots at free-kicks became obvious.

On the hour Sinclair played a one-two with substitute Vialli and screwed a good chance wide. Sinclair was like a midfielder. Chelsea were playing 2–4–4. No-one knew where they were. Nothing happened.

For the last ten minutes Duberry went to centre-forward and his header from Le Saux's cross was brilliantly tipped away by Martyn. But it was Chelsea's only bit of thunder. As the whistle neared they never looked like breaking through. They had thirteen second-half off-target shots, most hit wimpishly from outside the penalty area. Leeds celebrated as if they had won. And in a way they had.

So what was it? Was it lack of fight? Was it a sudden lack of belief around the penalty area? Was it lack of width, or lack of pace in front of defence? Was it lack of shape? Organization? Or was it just one of those things?

Blackburn moved up to second and Chelsea fell to third.

	Chelsea	Leeds
Shots on target	4	0
Corners	16	0
Fouls	12	19
Offsides	6	9
Bookings	3	3

Di Matteo, pushing (19), Wise, tangling (24), Nicholls, foul (39); Radebe on Zola (5), Robertson on Petrescu (26), Ribeiro on Le Saux (32).

Sendings off	0	2

Haaland, two bookings, kick out at Di Matteo (19), retaliation on Wise (24), Kelly, two bookings, refusing to withdraw at corner (1), foul on Leboeuf (45).

> ❝We had nobody to mark up front so people want to get forward, the crowd want us to bomb on forward. We say stay cool, pass the ball around and the opening will smack you in the face. We didn't do that well enough. We threw Michael Duberry up, but really we didn't make the most of him because we're not used to lumping balls into the box or looking for little knock downs.❞
>
> Graham Rix

	Chelsea	Leeds
Goals	0	0

Saturday 20 December
Hillsborough
28,334

Sheffield Wednesday 1 Chelsea 4
RECORD WIN AT HILLSBOROUGH

So how would Chelsea cope? Defeats at Coventry, Bolton and Blackburn could be swept aside with 'if only we had put away our chances,' and against Arsenal and Liverpool with 'if only we'd had eleven men'. The draw with Leeds was more confidence threatening.

Wednesday had just suffered a 1–0 reverse at West Ham on the back of four successive victories under the new management of Ron Atkinson, who, with former Chelsea coach Peter Shreeves, was steering them out of relegation trouble.

Gullit didn't panic after Leeds. He gave Vialli the chance up front and he quietly brought Kharine onto the substitutes' bench as

Championship material again. And as against Tromsø and in the second-half at Tottenham, every on-target shot went in.

It started off unbelievably frustratingly with Zola set free by Wise after two minutes, but the maestro mysteriously scuffed his shot. Wednesday had a chance a quarter of an hour later after Nicholls had fouled Di Canio wide. Di Canio's free-kick gave Booth an unchallenged header which he put over.

Luck ridden, Chelsea took the lead just before the half hour. Wednesday old boy Petrescu, booed every time he touched the ball, took possession off Vialli who was running square along the eighteen-yard line and ran the other way before releasing an angled

Vialli wins a penalty off Nolan

Hitchcock was injured. Kharine had been out since September 1996 when he suffered a ruptured cruciate ligament at the same ground.

There was no need to be anxious. Gullit's cool proved justified. Chelsea created chances from the beginning, managed to miss a couple of sitters, be denied two blatant penalties and still win by a wonderful margin.

All the style came flooding back. They looked real

shot through a crowd back into the far corner. The build-up had been excellent with Leboeuf winning possession and Di Matteo flying forward. Petrescu kept his celebration low-key in front of those Wednesday fans.

That goal brought confidence streaming back. Anything was possible now.

Vialli, racing on to Zola's pass, appeared to be brought down by

Sheffield Wednesday

Pressman

Nolan   Newsome   Walker   Stefanovic

Whittingham   Collins   Rudi   Pembridge
(Hyde 58)

Di Canio   Booth
(Carbone 67)

Referee: **Graham Barber** (Pyrford, Surrey)

Vialli   Zola
(Flo 67)

Di Matteo
Nicholls   Petrescu
Wise

Le Saux   Leboeuf   Duberry   Sinclair
(Clarke 76)

de Goey

Chelsea

Nolan three minutes before half-time but the referee waved play on. Three minutes after half-time a marvellous move involving half the team ended with Collins clearly holding Vialli. Again there was no penalty award.

Just before that Vialli had slammed over when he had all the time in the world following Leboeuf's fine free-kick.

Chelsea needed a second goal to reflect their domination and make the game safe. Once again you wondered if it might not come when old England defender Walker superbly raced across to block Petrescu's angled blast. But from Zola's resulting corner Vialli nipped in front of Pressman and headed home his eleventh goal of the season and his first League goal since the Barnsley game.

Seven minutes later Vialli finally won his penalty, running onto Leboeuf's pass, allowing Nolan to catch up and then turning him in the area. It looked a bit of an easy fall, and the complaining Nolan was booked.

Ron Atkinson didn't complain. 'Of the three penalty shouts they had, I thought the one they got had least claim to it,' was all he said. An admission by any other name. Leboeuf drove the kick under Pressman.

Chelsea then got lazy. Job done, 3–0 up. Except, there were thirty minutes to go and the job wasn't done. Pembridge, too often a scourge of Chelsea, was allowed to drive one in from twenty-five yards. Then Wise and Sinclair got hot under the collar with each other over

Sinclair's positioning and the full-back failed to cool down. He crashed into Hyde with a two-footed tackle, was booked, and that meant that, like Wise, he was suspended for the FA Cup tie with Manchester United. Gullit immediately substituted him.

Flo had come on for Zola, however, and quickly got into his 'supersub' act. First he dribbled sensationally past three defenders and squared the ball across an open goal only just in front of Nicholls. And then, after Di Matteo had snatched the ball from Wednesday, Flo ran threateningly for twenty-five yards before somehow hitting a curler from the centre of play that arched out and then in low at Pressman's left-hand post without the goalkeeper having a chance. Flo's top piece of brilliance so far.

Third place, five points behind leaders Manchester United. Confidence restored.

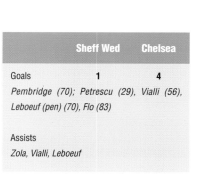
Vialli heads Chelsea's second

> *People say you can't lose seven games and win the Championship. This is nonsense. Football is all about winning games. A draw is like losing, you get just one point. We have won more games than anyone except Manchester United. I am happy. People complain about our defence too. Of course, you are always going to let in sloppy goals. But most weeks it doesn't happen. We have many clean sheets. I'm pleased.*
>
> **Ruud Gullit**

	Sheff Wed	Chelsea
Shots on target	4	4
Corners	3	7
Fouls	10	15
Offsides	11	2
Bookings	1	1

Nolan on Vialli (63); Sinclair, foul (75).

	Sheff Wed	Chelsea
Goals	1	4

Pembridge (70); Petrescu (29), Vialli (56), Leboeuf (pen) (70), Flo (83)

Assists
Zola, Vialli, Leboeuf

Friday 26 December
Stamford Bridge
34,529

Chelsea 1 Wimbledon 1

THE DAY THE MUSIC DIED

It happened at 12.27pm. Was it the turning point of just this game or of the Championship race? Or the entire season? Or, even, an era? It may well have been the latter. The game kicked off, as Boxing Day matches infuriatingly do in London, at midday. Wimbledon beat Chelsea on Boxing Day in 1995 despite Vinnie Jones being sent off. There was no chance of them winning now. They only had two shots all game. But Chelsea, having toyed with them for twenty-seven minutes, disintegrated and never really gelled again under Ruud Gullit's management.

There were peaks and troughs to come, but the art of domination by possession of the ball, of pass and fly, of annihilation of lesser teams, of scoring at crucial times, of defending a lead, died at 12.27pm.

Chelsea were leading 1–0. Once again Gullit had decided that Wimbledon would be Zola-obsessed and picked a team without him. His forwards had justified his decision after eight minutes. Flo chased an overhit cross wide to the left, bamboozled Blackwell and laid the ball back to Vialli who was sprinting towards him on a diagonal run. How Vialli kept control to wrong-foot goalkeeper Sullivan is a mystery, but nonetheless it was a superb finish.

Vialli dropped to his knees at Flo's feet in acknowledgement of his role in the goal, and Di Matteo joined him.

Chelsea ran the show after that although they had only a Flo shot to show for it. It wasn't penetrating, which was irritating at times, but it was all Chelsea. Until 12.27pm.

Then Frank Sinclair underhit a back-pass to de Goey and Michael Hughes nipped in to equalize.

It shouldn't have mattered. It should have been a blip in a confident team's path to three points. It wouldn't have mattered earlier in the season. And to be fair, nine minutes later, Di Matteo seemed to have restored the lead with his close-range piledriver from Le Saux's pull back, but Sullivan produced a brilliant tip-over. That was it. No more shots, no more moves, no more shape, no more pattern of play.

It was unfortunate on Sinclair who had been having an excellent season. There were fans who questioned his place in the team, but that was rubbish. Sinclair is a Chelsea hero. It is a sad fact that fans take longer to love a homegrown player than they do a signing.

Vialli and Di Matteo acknowledge Flo's assist

Chelsea

de Goey

Sinclair　　Duberry　　Leboeuf　　Granville
(Clarke 56)

Wise
Petrescu　　　　　　Le Saux
Di Matteo

Vialli　　Flo
(Zola 60)

*Referee: **Gary Willard** (Worthing)*

Gayle
(Cort 66)

Michael Hughes　Earle　Jones　Solbakken　Ardley

Kimble　Thatcher　Blackwell　Cunningham

Sullivan

Wimbledon

Sinclair had over 200 Chelsea games behind him and had been first choice for managers Ian Porterfield, David Webb, Glenn Hoddle and now Ruud Gullit. He had played in two Cup Finals and was about to star in another final. His game may be all about pace and strength, but when improvement was required to live with the imports, he provided it.

He came back from the 1994 FA Cup Final defeat and absurd penalty decision against him to score the first goal the following season. He had character. He wasn't a world beater but he was a Chelsea star.

Yet he was now at a low ebb. He had been selected by Jamaica with the World Cup coming up after their manager had watched Chelsea's 4-0 win over Derby, and his focus seemed to fall away. He started doing stupid things.

Wimbledon manager Joe Kinnear was surprised and delighted. 'It was always going to be difficult coming to a place like Chelsea, especially the form that they're in. To go behind that early, you fear the worst. They were at their best then. I thought we'd have the extra man in midfield knowing they had Wise and Di Matteo. They like to pass in triangles in that sort of area, so it was a case of having an extra player in there and one less striker.'

But after the equalizer the triangles stopped. 'They certainly played a different game to what they normally do against us,' Kinnear confirmed. 'They hit a lot of diagonal balls from both centre-halves. We knew that the players on the pitch who would have the ball most would be their centre-halves, and we tried to make it that Duberry had it more than Leboeuf. We didn't think he could hurt us from that area. In the end we more or less forced them to hit long balls.'

Gullit tried to explain the loss of belief. 'When you give away a goal like that, I think that broke us down a little bit. It was a very vital moment. It was a moment that you could go two-, three-zero. It was just sloppy. Before they equalized we played well. The frustration is that they didn't even create one chance. If you don't give that chance away they never would score a goal.'

Then he delivered his normal 'optimism and total belief' conclusion. 'Last year they said these games we would lose easily. Now we don't even give a chance away.' But he allowed his own frustration to show. 'But the second-half we didn't create a chance.'

For the second home game running an opposition backing off and defending with their lives killed Chelsea's attacking force. When Chelsea were given space they needed pace, the turns and the one-touch and the pass and fly didn't take them away from markers. When the game was spread out they were reduced to playing long balls.

Zola came on for Vialli after an hour. The crowd booed the fact that Vialli was going off. He had, as ever, been boxing clever, and it was noticeable that Flo's game fell away with the substitution. Zola was again disappointing, becoming the off-form player the media were describing.

Was it something that had been building up since Blackburn away? Or since Leeds a fortnight before? Or did it just happen here?

Seven points behind the leaders now. For the first time there seemed to be doubt in the players' minds.

> *Maybe we try to play the killer ball a bit too early. But teams are just sitting back and getting men behind the ball, it's making things difficult for us. I think teams coming to Stamford Bridge are thinking the best they can do is get a draw. They're scared to play open football with us.*
>
> **Michael Duberry**

	Chelsea	Wimbledon
Shots on target	4	1
Corners	9	2
Fouls	9	16
Offsides	6	8
Bookings	0	3

Thatcher on Duberry (32), Michael Hughes on Petrescu (37), Kimble on Clarke (85).

	Chelsea	Wimbledon
Goals	1	1
Vialli (8); Hughes (27)		
Assist		
Flo		

Monday 29 December
The Dell
15,231

Southampton 1 Chelsea 0
ANOTHER CHANCE TO CATCH UP MISSED

Chelsea knew that leaders Manchester United had lost and second placed Blackburn had only drawn at the weekend. A victory would put Chelsea back in second place, four points behind United.

In some ways Chelsea were unlucky to lose. Offside decisions went against them and Davies' goal was Southampton's only shot on target. But the nature of the defeat was in keeping with the new lack of confidence. Southampton were poor. This was the kind of opposition Chelsea had been annihilating a few weeks earlier.

Mark Hughes returned from suspension, but now Wise was suspended. Paul Hughes started his first game since September in his place. His was a strange selection as he had been out for over two months with a badly twisted ankle and had barely played since his return.

In defence Clarke returned for stomach upset victim Leboeuf. The absence of Leboeuf was a blow. Since Glenn Hoddle had taken over as manager in 1993, the Chelsea style was to pass from the back. But David Lee had not regained his old fitness and form following a broken leg and Gullit had let his own fitness slip sufficiently to rule himself out. So there was no natural playmaker in defence. The usual Chelsea pattern wasn't there.

Southampton played with a midfield three and Le Tissier free in front of them. Amazingly, Chelsea regularly failed to pick him up. How you can fail to pick up a renowned matchwinner when it is obvious he has the freedom of the park is a good question.

Early on, Petrescu raced forty yards into the Southampton penalty area but found no support. Three minutes later Davies scored his goal. It was unfair and avoidable. It was unfair because Palmer looked offside when he raced down the right on to Richardson's pass after Chelsea had cleared a corner. It was avoidable because when Sinclair lost the offside decision he sprinted back to cover Davies but allowed the forward to poke a toe

Mama Mia! *Zola wins a free-kick and prays for form*

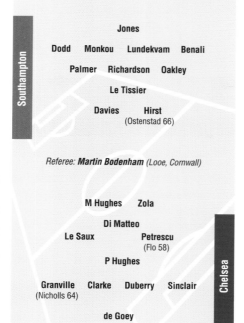

Southampton

Jones

Dodd   Monkou   Lundekvam   Benali

Palmer   Richardson   Oakley

Le Tissier

Davies   Hirst
(Ostenstad 66)

Referee: **Martin Bodenham** *(Looe, Cornwall)*

M Hughes   Zola

Di Matteo

Le Saux   Petrescu
(Flo 58)

P Hughes

Granville   Clarke   Duberry   Sinclair
(Nicholls 64)

de Goey

Chelsea

through his legs to get first touch to Palmer's poor cross.

Soon after Mark Hughes had a shot on the turn cleared off the line by Oakley, and Hughes was also to have a goal disallowed for offside. Again the decision looked harsh.

Southampton spurned two chances just before the interval. Davies ran on to Le Tissier's pass but shot wide as de Goey came out decisively, then Oakley got behind the defence to receive a pass but fired over.

There had been no cohesion, no pattern at all. There was battle, but there wasn't enough of it.

Early in the second-half a pathetic attempt to play offside allowed Hirst to race away after Southampton had cleared a dangerous Zola cross. Fortunately Davies ran offside to save Chelsea's blushes.

Attacking confusion was evident when Di Matteo put Sinclair away with a lovely ball, but on cutting in Sinclair powered in a dreadful low cross when a placed cut back would have found three Chelsea players steaming in. It wasn't Sinclair's month.

Southampton continued to create the chances with de Goey making a great save at Davies' feet and Hirst firing over as he followed up.

The appearance of Flo made a difference to Chelsea. He quickly turned away from a challenge and fired in low, bringing out a smart save from Jones. Then he headed a Zola free-kick just over.

Yet his entrance pushed Zola out to the right flank where he lost all effectiveness. Once again Zola's influence on the game seemed diminished.

The performance was summed up

	Southampton	Chelsea
Shots on target	1	5
Corners	2	4
Fouls	14	7
Offsides	8	7
Bookings	1	1

Palmer on Di Matteo (15); Le Saux, foul (45).

> *We've had a few problems in recent weeks chasing games and it turned out to be the same tonight. There was too much urgency. Later in the game when we were getting desperate we weren't showing the patience we were earlier in the season, we were snatching at half-chances, whereas earlier in the season we were making another pass and creating a proper chance. We've got to show a lot more patience.*
>
> Steve Clarke

seven minutes from time when more pathetic play by both sides – mis-hits, slices and complete misses – led to Le Saux's mis-hit shot which fell invitingly for Sinclair who ballooned over from close range.

Vialli came on for four minutes of stoppage time. The only serious action he witnessed was Southampton substitute Williams going past Le Saux, Nicholls and Duberry before shooting wide.

For the second game running Gullit was finding it difficult to hide his frustration. 'We throw the game away in the first-half and then you try to repair something and in the second-half you have more control, you create more chances, but it doesn't fall for you and the more you wait the more strong the opposition is going to get. It is stupid.' Then came his 'optimism and total belief' conclusion: 'They know it themselves and that is good,' but once again he couldn't maintain it, 'but it is a great opportunity that you throw away. You prepare them and they know what they had to do and then they did exactly the opposite and that is what makes you angry.'

Southampton manager Dave Jones couldn't hide his satisfaction after his side's two defeats at Stamford Bridge. 'We went there in the Coca-Cola and we learnt an awful lot and I just felt we had to close them down as far away from goal as possible.'

So Leeds and Wimbledon backed off. Southampton pushed up and closed down. No goals, few chances. Still third, but Gullit's first real difficult patch as manager had arrived. One win in four was not the stuff of champions. And three 1–0 defeats in six away games wasn't the Gullit style for his Chelsea.

	Southampton	Chelsea
Goals	1	0

Davies (15)

Sunday 4 January
Stamford Bridge
34,792

Chelsea 3 Manchester United 5

LATE GOALS COVER UP CHELSEA SHAME AND ANNIHILATION

This was the most keenly anticipated game throughout the nation – the FA Cup holders defending their trophy against the Premiership champions. The squad that Gullit had built was definitely the most entertaining and possibly the most serious challenger to United's crown. It turned into a match of utter shame and annihilation for Chelsea, who were 5–0 down with thirteen minutes to go. Yet in a mad finish they could have nicked a draw.

Chelsea's build-up was as shambolic as their performance. They took everything bad from the last few games and magnified it in this fixture.

But the whole affair has to be put in perspective. In some respects the game wasn't that important to either Gullit or United manager Ferguson.

generation anyway, and it was a big stage, so he focused on that too. In fact, he was being like Alex Ferguson.

Ferguson laughed after his side's victory: 'Neither of us wanted a replay. We can't afford it. I told Schmeichel that if it was a draw with ten minutes to go he was going up front, no problem.'

United, of course, held the European Champions' League at the top of their priorities with the Premiership second. But Ferguson couldn't prevent the nation's and the media's attention getting to his team as he admitted afterwards. 'They were really up for it. The FA Cup is such a big competition and Chelsea are a good team. They didn't want to lose this.'

Everything went wrong for Chelsea. Wise and Sinclair were suspended. Babayaro and Poyet were injured and, most

Clarke's pressure prevents Cole from opening the scoring

Gullit's priorities were the League and Europe. He had won the Cup. He liked new adventures. And he only wanted to compete with the best. That meant qualifying for the European Champions' League, 'the Cup with big ears,' as he called it. The European Cup Winners' Cup was a new stage to conquer, for this Chelsea

importantly, so was Newton, who would have replaced Wise.

After Southampton on the Monday the team trained on New Year's Eve, and then Gullit flew off to Amsterdam for New Year. He returned on the Friday with flu symptoms, but attended training at Stamford Bridge. There, behind closed doors, the squad played an

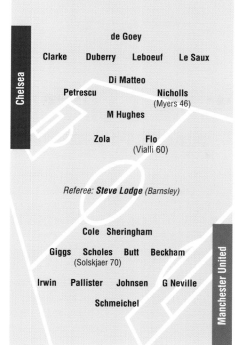

de Goey

Clarke   Duberry   Leboeuf   Le Saux

Di Matteo

Petrescu   Nicholls
(Myers 46)

M Hughes

Zola   Flo
(Vialli 60)

Referee: **Steve Lodge** (Barnsley)

Cole   Sheringham

Giggs   Scholes   Butt   Beckham
(Solskjaer 70)

Irwin   Pallister   Johnsen   G Neville

Schmeichel

eleven-a-side practice match and he then chose his team.

He started the practice match with Clarke in Wise's midfield role and Paul Hughes at right-back. But that meant Hughes marking Giggs, and his form didn't look up to it. So they were switched. Clarke, obviously, was okay at right-back, he had spent much of his career there, but Hughes in the anchor midfield role still didn't seem strong enough. Lambourde wasn't considered.

So next Gullit brought Mark Hughes into midfield. He had played there for Wales and played the last twenty minutes there against Everton. He couldn't settle in an anchor role, so he was pushed to the front of the midfield diamond with Di Matteo dropping back to anchor the middle. Change after change.

Next day Gullit missed training but told Graham Rix which match-play sessions he wanted putting on.

On Sunday the match was kicking off at midday for television. Gullit decided at the last moment to attend but did not reveal the team to anyone until he got there, the team sheet being handed in to the referee at the last moment. It was as training had finished.

Ferguson looked at the sheet and assumed Chelsea were going for win or bust.

Beckham scored the first goal midway through the first-half when Leboeuf couldn't stop Cole crossing; he also scored the second direct from a free-kick after a Nicholls foul, Sheringham pulling Petrescu out of the wall as Beckham

stroked the ball past a disbelieving and stumbling de Goey; Cole scored the third right on half-time, outsprinting Leboeuf before beating de Goey from an acute angle. Giggs had played a crucial role in all three goals. Only Di Matteo wasn't struggling.

Gullit sent on Myers for Nicholls at half-time and switched to 3–4–3. Le Saux immediately became more effective, hitting the bar with an angled volley after five minutes, Schmeichel saving Zola's follow-up. But two more goals came: Giggs sent Cole away again between Duberry and Leboeuf to finish easily, and then Sheringham was given a free header following a short corner.

It was diabolical. Zola was having his worst game ever, so was Leboeuf and Flo was again anonymous. There was nothing encouraging anywhere on the pitch.

But Le Saux chipped a beautiful consolation goal four minutes after Sheringham's header. There were still thirteen minutes to go. Suddenly Vialli took over. He had come on for Flo on the hour. He raced onto Petrescu's pass to volley past Schmeichel with seven minutes left. Two minutes later Di Matteo was agonizingly and fractionally wide when through. What if that had gone in? Two minutes later Vialli read Pallister's negligent pass back and worked Chelsea's third goal with Petrescu. But the miracle stopped there.

Ferguson was happy. 'You have to give credit to Chelsea, they kept going. They got something out of the game which saves a big embarrassment to them. But it was our day.'

And so it was. On the day it didn't really matter to Gullit. In time, it would.

> *They were stronger than we were today. They played a great game. You can't make one mistake because they punish you. You can't concede so many goals to a big team like Manchester United. We're going to show them what we can do in the League when we have all our players. We gave our best but it wasn't enough.*
>
> **Roberto Di Matteo**

	Chelsea	Man Utd
Shots on target	5	9
Woodwork	1	0
Corners	4	7
Fouls	20	17
Offsides	4	3
Bookings	5	3

Hughes, foul (20), Nicholls, foul (27), Di Matteo, not withdrawing (38), Leboeuf, foul (64), Le Saux, bust-up (90); Irwin on Hughes (23), Scholes on Clarke (68); Sheringham, bust-up with Le Saux (90).

	Chelsea	Man Utd
Goals	3	5

Le Saux (77), Vialli (83, 87); Beckham (22, 27), Cole (45, 65), Sheringham (73)

Assists	

Petrescu 2

Wednesday 7 January
Portman Road
22,088

Ipswich 2 Chelsea 2
CHELSEA WON 4–1 ON PENALTIES

Chelsea were now the centre of attention for a new reason. And the media's special focus was on Ruud Gullit. The biggest superstar in English football, the habitual winner who had brought silverware to Stamford Bridge for the first time in twenty-six years, was presiding over a team that seemed to be falling apart.

Gullit remained calm and untouched on the surface. He reminded the media that he knew all about the pressures of winning, and especially the pressures brought on you after winning. Once you have done it you have to keep doing it. You have to work through the bad periods and come out winning and confident.

'We have reached a new period of pressure which people have to

that the Football League would be successful in making UEFA retain a place in their tournament for the Coca-Cola winners. It could be that the eight teams left were battling for a European spot.

Manchester United manager Alex Ferguson had laughed on Sunday when asked about pressure of games and whether he felt Chelsea didn't wish that they had been knocked out of the Coca-Cola like United. 'Well, they kept on trying, didn't they, they kept fielding their reserve team.'

If any of the media pressure was stinging Gullit the most, it was their charge that he was wrong not to play himself on Sunday when the team needed him. This was harsh as he was very low with a cold. Now he put himself on the bench.

De Goey saves the first penalty

deal with. No longer if you lose at Chelsea is it okay. People don't say that anymore. "Oh well, there's always next week." Now we have to get used to new pressures. We are expected to win all our games.'

He was right. And he was fortunate to find himself in a winner's position in the Coca-Cola Cup. Rumours had been gaining strength

And with Europe in the back of his mind, de Goey, Le Saux and Zola came in for their first Coca-Cola games of the season. Wise returned for his 300th Chelsea appearance, the twenty-sixth person to reach that milestone.

Gullit found himself on the pitch after twenty minutes when

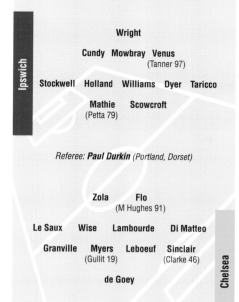

Ipswich

Wright

Cundy Mowbray Venus
(Tanner 97)

Stockwell Holland Williams Dyer Taricco

Mathie Scowcroft
(Petta 79)

Referee: **Paul Durkin** (Portland, Dorset)

Zola Flo
(M Hughes 91)

Le Saux Wise Lambourde Di Matteo

Granville Myers Leboeuf Sinclair
(Gullit 19) (Clarke 46)

de Goey

Chelsea

Myers tore a hamstring. Ipswich were beginning to get up a head of steam to climb from the lower reaches of Division One to a play-off position. Gullit quickly found his passion.

He was noticeably unfit, lacking pace and sharpness, and the quality of his passing was below his usual standard. But his strength of character and will to win were massive. When Sinclair declined a simple pass back to him and tried to turn his winger, running the ball carelessly into touch, he screamed for a substitution. On another occasion he gestured angrily for Sinclair to move forward for a pass.

The Chelsea pattern of earlier in the season still wasn't there, and he was frustrated that more wasn't being done to recreate it.

All the same, Chelsea ambled into a two-goal lead. Just after the half-hour Leboeuf's long pass attracted Wright from his goal when he should have stayed on his line. Le Saux lobbed a cross over him and Flo won the race to net the ball. Gullit then got stuck on an upfield foray allowing Stockwell to counter and de Goey had to save with his feet after the wing-back had gone past Granville. But Chelsea hit a fabulous second when Zola jumped over Gullit's diagonal ball and kept running to receive Flo's pass into space. Zola crossed first time and Le Saux, all alone, netted. All one-touch.

However, Chelsea immediately conceded. Leboeuf was by-passed by Mathie and although de Goey palmed away the resulting shot Taricco turned up to score from the angle.

At half-time Sinclair was replaced.

Clarke proudly came on for his 400th Chelsea appearance. He is only the eighth person to achieve this feat.

But just after the hour Chelsea gave away a stupid equalizer. Le Saux lost possession from Gullit's pass, and Gullit failed to get back. The forward he was marking, Mathie, converted Stockwell's cross.

Chelsea never looked like losing and could have won when old boy Cundy smacked a Di Matteo cross against his own bar. Wise seemed impeded when he was brought down in the area right on time, but the referee waved play on.

Extra time was quiet as the teams looked tired. Gullit could barely run, but still managed to lope out a long leg and hook the ball back from two marauding Ipswich forwards before placing a pass to a colleague. Ipswich could have nicked the semi-final place when Petta jinked through with eight minutes to go but he hit the post when he should have scored.

And so to another penalty shoot-out. Chelsea certainly were proceeding the hard way in this tournament. Wise limped off, his toe and ankle too swollen to take another kick. De Goey brilliantly palmed away Scowcroft's low shot to his left, Ipswich's first kick, and then easily saved Taricco's weak effort to his right, Ipswich's third kick.

Chelsea won without missing. And before they had changed they heard they had a semi-final draw with Arsenal. Suddenly the Coca-Cola Cup was big time.

Last four for Europe? Who was worried about League form!

> We should have had two penalties. the game should have been over and won. We played well in patches and we gave them two not very good goals. We were cruising two up and we gave them a sloppy goal in the forty-fifth minute which gave them a buzz for the second-half. Big Ed is big enough for penalties, he'll frighten the life out of you. It's great to see me and Clarkey still here, 700 games between us and into another semi-final.
>
> Dennis Wise

	Ipswich	Chelsea
Shots on target	7	3
Woodwork	1	1
Corners	6	2
Fouls	17	8
Offsides	3	9
Bookings	1	1

Cundy on Flo(32); Leboeuf, foul (24).

	Ipswich	Chelsea
Goals	2	2

Taricco (45), Mathie (61); Flo (31), Le Saux(45)

Assists

Leboeuf, Le Saux, Zola, Flo

	Ipswich	Chelsea
Penalties	1	4

Leboeuf, Scowcroft (saved), Zola, Tanner, Di Matteo, Taricco (saved), M Hughes

Saturday 10 January
Stamford Bridge
34,647

Chelsea 3 Coventry City 1
THE LEGACY OF GLENN HODDLE RESURRECTED

Let's face it, Chelsea were still in contention. Gullit was right. Things were good. When could the Blues last have boasted of being in the top three in January and still in the Championship race? 1986 maybe. Otherwise you have to go back to the 1960s.

Coventry were on a good run. In their last game they had knocked Liverpool out of the FA Cup at Anfield, and in the game before that they had beaten Manchester United at home. Chelsea had a debt to repay after losing the first League game of the season at Highfield Road.

Petrescu had flu and Vialli a stitched hand so both were unavailable. Vialli's hand had been trodden on in the Wimbledon game and the wound had re-opened in the Manchester United match. Sinclair was again suspended. Long-term injuries were Newton, who started full training in the morning, Poyet, Babayaro and now Myers.

Lambourde had been recalled at Ipswich for his first game since the previous Coca-Cola round, and his athletic performance earned him another chance.

Supplier Le Saux and scorer Nicholls

There had been no thought in Gullit's mind of a change of approach after the Christmas defeats and FA Cup murder. 'We've played our shape, we've played it all season, and we're not going to change it,' he said.

That shape was a back four, a midfield four either in a diamond formation or flatter and more solid, and a front two. He had

changed during games, of course, most notably at half-time against United. He was to change again today. The formation question was a strong debating point amongst Chelsea followers.

It had started with Glenn Hoddle in 1993 when he arrived to re-introduce stylish football. He installed a 3–5–2 formation straight away with himself as sweeper and Steve Clarke and Andy Dow as wing-backs, and, surprisingly, Mal Donaghy as the midfield anchor. By Boxing Day Chelsea were one off the bottom.

He switched to a back four with a midfield diamond and a front two, a formation he had the players for, and rocketed away from relegation and straight to the FA Cup Final which also brought European qualification.

But he set the club up to play 3–5–2 along his single-minded footballing lines. The first team stuck to their formation the next season, and by November were through to the last eight in Europe and into the top eight in the Premiership. But League form dropped, and after an unsatisfactory attempt at 3–5–2, with a back three of Johnsen, Sinclair and Kjeldbjerg, he finished the campaign with a solid 4–4–2, no diamonds, giving nothing away.

That summer he signed Gullit for sweeper. Clarke and now Myers or Scott Minto were the wing-backs. It was better, but it wasn't outstanding. Then in November he signed two wing-backs, Petrescu and Terry Phelan, made Lee sweeper and moved Gullit forward, and it was like an explosion. Chelsea had arrived. Up front he played his other new signing, Hughes, on his own, with two attacking midfielders just behind.

When Gullit took over he dispensed with the anchor midfielder and asked his three-man midfield to take responsibility on the pitch while being more liberated, to take their turns in making forward runs. And he always played two forwards. He signed Leboeuf to sweep and Vialli to partner Hughes. It was much better.

But he experimented, with 4–3–3 at Liverpool where Chelsea lost 5–1 and 4–3–3 at Sunderland where Chelsea lost 3–0. At one of the regular team meetings the players said that they felt that the team would be better off playing their own way and not switching formations so much. He took that on board, and against West Ham just before Christmas reverted to 3–5–2. It was, after all, the formation that allowed the likes of Duberry and Morris to come into the team from the reserves and youth squads and play the kind of football they were used to.

Chelsea's season took off with that game and they got back into Championship contention. The formation supported good wins against top teams: Manchester United away, Liverpool in the League and Cup at home, Aston Villa away.

But injuries to Kharine and Duberry left the defence weaker, and when Leboeuf was injured in the quarter-final of the FA Cup at

Chelsea

de Goey

Clarke   Duberry   Leboeuf   Granville
(Nicholls 46)

Lambourde

Wise   Le Saux

Di Matteo

M Hughes   Zola
(Gullit 59)

Referee: *Mike Reed* (Birmingham)

Coventry

Huckerby   Dublin

Whelan

Salako   Telfer
(Moldovan 57)

Boland

Burrows   Williams   Breen   Shaw

Hedman

Portsmouth, shape was lost. Lee and Gullit were also injured and there was no natural sweeper. By the time Leboeuf came back Gullit was ready to change to a back four for the FA Cup semi-final against Wimbledon.

There was a strong feeling in the management camp that that was the way you had to play to win things. And who could argue. The results would prove it.

But with sweeper Leboeuf, wing-backs Petrescu, Le Saux and Babayaro, and players coming through the ranks practiced in 3–5–2, many felt the team was built by Hoddle to play that way, and nothing had changed. The results came because Chelsea had good players. But they didn't come against top teams.

Chelsea didn't have a useless first-half against Coventry. Le Saux was denied by Hedman when he produced a diving header. But Huckerby missed a golden chance just before the half hour and Chelsea's confidence dived. Three minutes later Telfer took advantage of Granville missing Salako's deflected cross after Duberry had lost possession to score.

At half-time Gullit brought on Nicholls and switched to 3–5–2. Immediately everything was better. He took off Zola, again in poor form, and came on himself, making positive runs. In no time Le Saux supplied two crosses for Nicholls to hare forward from midfield and score his first home goals, one a header, the other a left-footed diversion. The second Le Saux break came from a perfectly delivered Lambourde pass which took out four Coventry players.

Coventry had switched to 4–3–3 to try and get at Chelsea's back line, so Chelsea now switched back to 4–4–2

with Lambourde at right-back. Leboeuf was still spare. Quickly, Nicholls' ball into the box was stepped over by Hughes for Di Matteo to sweep in the third. Almost immediately Gullit had an effort well turned round.

The change was extraordinary. The electricity, the pattern, the passing, the flying were back. And Gullit, despite his huff and puff, had made a difference with his cameo appearance.

But how should Chelsea play now? And why was everyone debating it? Chelsea were now up to second.

Nicholls volleying Chelsea into the lead

	Chelsea	Coventry
Shots on target	5	2
Corners	11	2
Fouls	14	16
Offsides	2	6
Bookings	2	3

Duberry, foul (9), Clarke, foul (39), Salako on Clarke (5), Huckerby on Leboeuf (15), Dublin on Le Saux (37).

Graham Rix shouted out about three minutes before I scored: "Get in the box, how are you supposed to score from where you are?" Graeme's then put two great crosses in for me and he put another one in with about ten minutes to go which I should have done better with. Playing with a 3–5–2 I found more space in midfield than I would in a four.

Mark Nicholls

	Chelsea	Coventry
Goals	3	1

Nicholls (66, 69), Di Matteo (77); Telfer (30)

Assists
M Hughes 2, Le Saux 2, Lambourde, Nicholls

Sunday 18 January
Goodison Park
32,355

Everton 3 Chelsea 1

NO WISE, NO WIN

Despite the bad run, Chelsea had lost only two of the last ten games. They were the two games which Dennis Wise had missed. Gullit pulled another team selection surprise out of his bag just before kick-off when he announced that Wise would not be playing. He sprang the decision that if he could not train, he could not continue playing.

The agreement that the physio staff should get him fit for each match had not been discussed again, and the decision was a surprise. Wise had travelled up in the squad expecting to play and was as shocked as anyone.

It was especially surprising as Di Matteo was suspended following his booking against Manchester United. Instead, Lambourde was partnered in midfield by Newton, back in training following his injury.

Gullit also left Zola out. Zola's form had completely drained, but it was another shock when he wasn't even on the bench. Zola accepted it gracefully.

But it was decided to tell the media about Wise's injury, although the extent of its history wasn't revealed, and to avoid the headlines that Zola's axing would bring, he was said to be suffering from a stomach upset.

Blackburn had gone up to second the day before with a draw, so victory would confirm Chelsea in second place. Manchester United were playing on Monday night.

Everton were still in the relegation zone and played like it. Chelsea won five first-half corners to their none, but didn't particularly threaten the goal. The solid 4–4–2 formation gave strength but not a lot of creativity.

Lambourde was increasing in confidence, but poor Newton was nowhere near match fitness. The few good positions that were gained were never developed near the penalty area.

Only one side, however, was likely to take the lead, and Chelsea did it nine minutes before half-time. As against Coventry, Lambourde's pass opened up the opposition, finding his left-back,

Le Saux finds it one against two as Everton inflict another defeat

Everton

Myrhre

Short **Bilic** **Tiler**
(Thomsen 87)

Allen **Grant** **Speed** **Ball**

Barmby

Madar **Ferguson**
(Farrelly 70)

*Referee: **Alan Wilkie** (Chester-le-Street)*

M Hughes **Flo**
(Vialli 69)

Le Saux **Newton** **Lambourde** **Petrescu**

Clarke **Leboeuf** **Duberry** **Sinclair**
(Gullit 73)

de Goey

Chelsea

Clarke. Clarke's left-foot cross into the danger zone was seized upon by Flo who used his strength to hold off Tiler, then turned tarantula-like upon the loose ball to bury it. An excellent striker's goal. Flo was increasingly looking like a top goalscorer.

Inexplicably, Chelsea threw it away within two minutes. Barmby left Newton behind and crossed from the right, and in the mayhem de Goey flicked the ball on and away beyond the far post. Madar headed it back but Sinclair covered to clear off the line, yet Speed had been left by Petrescu as he made a twenty-five-yard run for the cross and was free to equalize from an acute angle.

No wonder Gullit was angry. 'We controlled the game, played some good football, then gave a goal away unnecessarily.'

When the teams came out for the second-half, Chelsea's confidence was gone. Accident followed accident. There were no leaders to save the slippage.

De Goey was left stranded by an early free-kick but Leboeuf cleared from the line. Petrescu hit an abysmal corner to Leboeuf on the edge of the area, he was dispossessed by Allen who raced the length of the pitch but failed to get a shot on goal. Ferguson caused trouble with his aggression and Madar nearly benefited, de Goey saving superbly with his legs.

But from the resulting corner Duberry lost Ferguson, leaving him with a free header eight yards out. The effort carried little venom but went under de Goey's dive. Everton started to believe in themselves.

Grant had a thirty-yarder which de Goey palmed away and Chelsea never threatened to retaliate. So Gullit brought himself on for Sinclair and reverted to 3–4–3. His early crossfield pass for another substitute, Vialli, brought a shot that was just wide, but Chelsea had no petrol in the tank, no belief.

With eight minutes to go Barmby delivered a series of dummies all willingly bought in midfield, and although Duberry, running into his own area diagonally, allowed Ferguson first touch on Farrelly's pass, he accelerated ahead of him to defend. Unfortunately he then slashed the ball past de Goey for an undignified own goal. Everton were coasting.

There remained time for Ferguson to send another free header straight at de Goey and for Speed almost to break in two the near post when he crashed a drive against the top of it.

Gullit was so angry. 'Second-half, I won't even mention the goals we gave away. The thing that irritates you more is that we gave the ball away all the time. You don't deserve to be at this level if you play like that.'

It was one of Chelsea's poorest performances of the season. But Manchester United lost on Monday night, so there were still only seven points separating them from the leaders. It should have been four. It should have been even fewer over the last few weeks.

On Tuesday night Liverpool won their game in hand and Chelsea dropped to fourth.

> *We have been struggling lately, so it is good for us that there is a ten day break to the next match. I was very satisfied when I scored but it didn't help the team. We should be more concentrated when we score. We didn't create very much.*
>
> **Tore Andre Flo**

	Everton	Chelsea
Shots on target	6	1
Woodwork	1	0
Corners	3	7
Fouls	7	10
Offsides	7	2
Bookings	1	2

Short on M Hughes (76); Lambourde, foul (23), M Hughes, kick out (76).

	Everton	Chelsea
Goals	3	1

Speed (38), Ferguson (61), Duberry (o.g.) (82); Flo (36)

Assists
Lambourde, Clarke

Wednesday 28 January
Highbury
38,114

Arsenal 2 Chelsea 1

HUGHES GOAL GETS CHELSEA OUT OF JAIL

Every League game was big time. Every Cup game was big time. This is what Gullit had brought to Chelsea. But the pressures were increasing. In possibly the most stupid Club v Country conflict to date, Leboeuf and Di Matteo were called away for international friendlies claimed by their countries to be important pre-World Cup games. Arsenal's Vieira was also required.

No matter that this was a major Cup semi-final in which, increasingly, it looked like the ultimate winners would qualify for Europe. Added to the farce was the fact that Leboeuf finished up making a two minute substitute appearance for France. At least Di Matteo started and scored for Italy.

he was so much better than everybody else. That's not to say he didn't take his career seriously or look after his body properly – he did all the right things for him. But he had treated this season like a manager would and not done the right things as a player.

In another packed, tension-filled stadium, on another night of live television broadcasting, in another crunch match, Chelsea were appalling. They just never got going.

Zola was recalled. Wise wasn't. No Wise, no win. Newton dredged up all his knowledge and experience to give an excellent battling midfield performance which was just as well because it was one game too many for Lambourde in the midfield. He, remember, came to Chelsea as a central defender who had played half-a-dozen

Outnumbered, Zola is gunned down at Highbury

So Gullit was robbed of his defensive playmaker. He decided to play himself. This was his first start ever in a major game at centre-back. You wouldn't have called the earlier Coca-Cola matches major games.

It was a decision he said he had to take. 'There was no-one else.' It was one which was to rebound on him.

His lack of training caught up with him. Throughout his life Gullit the player had been able to do largely as he pleased because

games in midfield during his career.

Arsenal dominated. De Goey was magnificent. The goalkeeper who had started the season so meekly was a giant between the sticks. The tallest man ever to play for Chelsea gave the first of a series of outstanding Cup displays that were to take Chelsea to glory.

In the roundabout of personnel to fill the left-sided problem area, Clarke continued at left-back with Le Saux in midfield.

Poor Sinclair at right-back kept finding himself all alone with three

Arsenal

Manninger

Grimandi   Adams   Bould   Winterburn
(Platt 84)

Parlour   Petit   S Hughes   Overmars

Anelka   Bergamp

Referee: **Martin Bodenham** (Looe, Cornwall)

Flo   Zola
(M Hughes 59)

Le Saux   Lambourde   Newton   Petrescu
(Charvet 46)

Clarke   Gullit   Duberry   Sinclair
(Vialli 86)

de Goey

Chelsea

Arsenal players bearing down on him. There was no cover from Gullit, Petrescu or Duberry. Arsenal lined up the chances.

Newton raced back to tackle striker Anelka when Clarke and Gullit were struggling. De Goey saved well to his left from Parlour's twenty-five-yarder. Bergkamp got away from Gullit to head Winterburn's cross against the bar. Stephen Hughes' ripping twenty-yarder was parried and held at the second attempt by de Goey.

Chelsea finally broke midway through the first half and it was Gullit who snapped. Petit's basic lob forward had the player-manager backing off to head, but the spring in his legs wasn't there, and his backward effort never reached de Goey. Overmars sprinted in to stab home.

Newton had harsh words for his boss, but the boss spat them back. Chelsea held on until the interval when it was clear there had to be changes.

The changes were surprising. Chelsea switched to 3–5–2, but rather than use Petrescu at wing-back, he was substituted and Laurent Charvet made his debut. Charvet had just been signed on loan from Cannes until the end of the season to see how effective he was.

The first thing that happened was that Overmars got in behind him and Newton and crossed for Stephen Hughes to score his first goal of the season. The tie looked lost.

Tempers were on overheat. Le Saux, booked just before half-time, was fouled by Grimandi, and got so blindly angry that he was lucky not to be sent off.

	Arsenal	Chelsea
Shots on target	9	1
Woodwork	1	0
Corners	8	3
Fouls	7	11
Offsides	4	4
Bookings	2	3

Bergkamp on Clarke (43), Grimandi on Le Saux (49); Le Saux, foul (42), Duberry, dissent (74), Newton, foul (85).

> *We've still got a good chance to go through to the final. When we played long balls, second ball was coming back immediately from them and gave us trouble in the back four, so we changed things at half-time. They press us very well and we have some problems with that, and they created a lot of chances but thank God they only score two. If we win 1–0 we go through. That's the only thing that matters.*
>
> **Ed de Goey**

Chelsea finally created a chance when Flo missed with a free header from Zola's corner. Zola was looking a little more perky than of late but Flo was struggling again. Mark Hughes replaced him.

After sixty-seven minutes de Goey saved the tie. Bergkamp, alone, hit a left-footed half-volley from fifteen yards to climax Anelka's counter-attack, and somehow the goalkeeper threw himself to his right and palmed it away. In quality it was a unique save. In timing it was invaluable.

Chelsea went straight down the other end, Zola crossed with the aid of a slight deflection, and Mark Hughes beat Manninger, in goal for the injured Seaman, to the ball to nod it past him. The old warhorse Hughes had saved another day.

Chelsea were better in the second-half. Gullit, in midfield, was less of a liability and produced moments of penetration and threat. Charvet did all right. But there was still no pattern. And the tempers were fraying.

But better play did not equal better results. Only de Goey ensured that. He brilliantly tipped over Petit's rising near-post drive and right on time caught Bergkamp's flighted twenty-yarder.

'I think the right score was 4–1,' said Arsenal manager Wenger. 'The Chelsea goalie made some great saves, he was fantastic.'

'We got out of jail,' admitted Gullit. But when he woke up to the newspapers next morning they were full of charges against him. Having demanded for the last few months, and especially the last few weeks, that he play, they were now demanding he hang up his boots.

	Arsenal	Chelsea
Goals	2	1

Overmars (22), S Hughes (46); M Hughes (68)

Assist		

Zola

Saturday 31 January
Stamford Bridge
34,442

Chelsea 2 Barnsley 0

UP TO SECOND, FOUR POINTS BEHIND LEADERS

It is my task to stand on the pitch with a microphone before the games at Stamford Bridge and make whatever announcements are required. Before today's game I drew everyone's attention to the League table. With second- and third-placed Liverpool and Blackburn playing each other, if Chelsea won we would definitely go third, and possibly second.

There was an unusual cheer of expectation. People truly believed that if Chelsea got things together they could still win the League. All around, the other teams were throwing it away as meekly as Chelsea. Whichever side was the first to put a run together could steal an advantage.

The day before, Friday, two days after defeat at Arsenal, Gullit held training behind closed doors at Stamford Bridge. He installed a 3–5–2 formation from the start. In his hour of need, he returned to what he had inherited. Charvet was to make his full debut at right wing-back and, with Di Matteo suspended, Petrescu played in midfield. Zola took his turn on the bench. Wise returned.

After training the players held a meeting in the dressing room to discuss their form and determine that having come this far, they were not going to throw the season away. From their point of view the meeting was not an irregular thing. Gullit had always encouraged discussion of all things football.

The boys celebrate Vialli's goal

de Goey

Duberry   **Leboeuf**   **Clarke**

Charvet   **Petrescu**   **Newton**   **Wise**   **Le Saux**
(Nicholls 46) (Sinclair 79)

Vialli   **M Hughes**

Referee: **Jeff Winter** *(Stockton-on-Tees)*

Ward   **Fjortoft**
(Hendrie 66)

Sheridan   **Redfearn**   **Bosancic**   **Bullock**
(Morgan 56)   (Liddell 80)

Barnard   **Moses**   **De Zeeuw**   **Eadie**

Watson

Barnsley

But waiting outside were the nation's media who had arrived for a regular pre-match press conference. They were alarmed at the idea of a players' meeting held without the manager, and stories of mutiny were written. They were wrong.

When was the last time Chelsea finished January with a game at home against the team one from the bottom in front of a full house? The side from Stamford Bridge was still the top attraction despite the last six weeks.

Chelsea won comfortably. Liverpool and Blackburn struggled to a goalless draw. And unbelievably, or maybe not for this season, Manchester United lost at home to Leicester. Chelsea rose not just to second, but to four points behind the leaders.

In the first minute Wise caught Barnsley's back line out and Vialli won a free-kick on the edge of the area which Le Saux slammed over. Duberry was booked early on. His confidence had dipped with Chelsea's shabby run and so had his performances. At twenty-two it was his first experience of individual pressure. A training ground explosion with Gullit the day before, nothing serious but nothing to further confidence, hadn't helped.

More helpful was the fifty-yard dash eight minutes before half-time which finished with Watson making a brave save at Vialli's feet.

Vialli had already put Chelsea ahead by then with his fifteenth goal of the season and his fifth against Barnsley. It was another of his clever slices across the goalkeeper with the outside of his right foot after an unchallenged Hughes had headed down Newton's cross. Barnsley

had a reputation for lovely play, but they were also lousy at defending.

Petrescu headed Le Saux's cross against the post after Watson had palmed away Le Saux's original shot five minutes before the interval, and then Wise, increasingly finding his bustling rhythm, played a one-two with Vialli before sidefooting wimpishly and allowing Watson to palm away. Chelsea should have been half way to another six by half-time.

Newton, finding two games in three days a burden, was replaced by the more attacking Nicholls at half-time. Hughes scored two minutes later from a move starting with de Goey. Wise and Vialli combined well, Petrescu crossed, Hughes screwed a header against the post and when the ball spun in the air he leapt up to head home.

It had been an emotional week, and after that Chelsea barely tried to drive home their advantage. Possession was protected, a clean sheet was safely ensured and coasting gear was all that was used. The 3–5–2 formation offered easy balance. Everyone looked comfortable.

Unfortunately the referee rather spoiled things with a profusion of yellow cards which caused Barnsley manager Danny Wilson to describe this as the worst refereeing performance he had seen all season. But he added: 'Let's not overshadow the performance from Chelsea first-half. They played very well. The amount of talent they've got they must stand a chance of the Championship.'

	Chelsea	Barnsley
Shots on target	6	3
Woodwork	2	0
Corners	6	6
Fouls	14	12
Offsides	6	10
Bookings	5	2

Duberry, foul (16), Le Saux, foul (32), Vialli, foul (71), Charvet, throwing the ball away (71), Petrescu, diving (88); Barnard on Vialli (9), Bosancic, dissent (55).

❝ *The team is slowly coming out of a difficult period. Yesterday we did a very difficult training session, a tactical training session. That demanded very much of the team. I had to do it. I had only one day to prepare all these things. That's why we faded a little bit in the last twenty minutes.* ❞

Ruud Gullit

	Chelsea	Barnsley
Goals	2	0

Vialli (22), M Hughes (47)

Assists

Newton, M Hughes, Vialli, Petrescu

Sunday 8 February
Highbury
38,083

Arsenal 2 Chelsea 0

ANOTHER CHANCE TO MOVE UP MISSED

Nothing is simple. No-one knew the significance of events unfolding. Another packed stadium, another tension-filled game, another live television broadcast. Training on Thursday had taken place at Stamford Bridge so another practice match could be staged behind closed doors. It appeared Gullit was sticking with 3–5–2. After all, the only victories since before Christmas had been achieved with this formation, against Coventry and Barnsley.

But Clarke suffered another calf strain before the match-play session, and with Myers still out, rather than use Granville Gullit reverted to a back four.

After the session he went to meet managing director Colin Hutchinson to discuss a new contract. It was a meeting Hutchinson had been trying to set up since October. Even now Gullit was keen on stalling. He didn't tell the board his reason, but it was to do with timing. He wanted to get the court case with his Italian wife over access to their children out of the way first.

He had recently confirmed he had no intention of leaving when his contract ran out in the summer. On *Clubcall* he had told Chelsea fans: 'People will try to force some kind of contract immediately. I already said we have a whole lot of things to do now. But I will stay. There is no problem. We just want to take our time because it's busy. The fans don't have to worry.'

But the board was getting worried. And when his meeting with Hutchinson moved nowhere forward after Hutchinson had said the club would no longer be prepared to pay him as a player-coach but only as a coach, and Gullit said he wanted two million pounds nett a year, moves began behind the scenes to replace him.

He was warned in the meeting that if he did not negotiate sensibly he would have to be replaced. He obviously considered

Goalkeeper Manninger catches Chelsea's only threat, a Charvet header

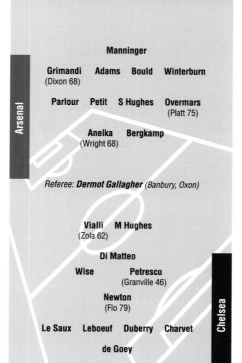

Manninger

Grimandi (Dixon 68)   **Adams**   **Bould**   **Winterburn**

Parlour   **Petit**   **S Hughes**   **Overmars** (Platt 75)

Anelka (Wright 68)   **Bergkamp**

Arsenal

*Referee: **Dermot Gallagher** (Banbury, Oxon)*

Vialli (Zola 62)   **M Hughes**

Di Matteo

Wise   **Petrescu** (Granville 46)

Newton (Flo 79)

Le Saux   **Leboeuf**   **Duberry**   **Charvet**

de Goey

Chelsea

this a bargaining position rather than a real threat. On the Saturday after training he telephoned Hutchinson to talk about new players, and Hutchinson repeated his warning. There was no response.

The Saturday went well for Chelsea. Manchester United only drew, while Liverpool and Blackburn both lost at home. A win would pull Chelsea away from third, fourth and fifth place – that was Arsenal – and leave them two points behind United with the leaders soon to come to Stamford Bridge.

The game, however, was another shapeless anti-climax. After two minutes Leboeuf was limping off melodramatically from a tough challenge. He returned to mis-hit a pass back which gave Anelka a run on goal. De Goey blocked, Duberry got back to tackle but couldn't clear, Charvet did but straight to Stephen Hughes who hit his second goal of the season from the edge of the box. His first had been against Chelsea.

Nothing is simple. When Petit mis-headed back towards his own penalty area, Vialli was the first to respond and raced clear on goal. Bould dragged him back on the edge of the penalty area. Tempers exploded – another top match, another soured atmosphere. Referee Gallagher chose to book Bould. 'I hoped for a yellow,' said Arsenal manager Wenger, 'and was scared he would give a red.'

'He has to be sent off,' said Gullit, 'there is no other rule for it. Everyone in the country applies that rule. It changed the whole game.'

It was a terrible decision. It was so bad that the FA suspended Gallagher for one game.

Parlour was booked for encroaching when the free-kick was

being lined up. Leboeuf's shot was deflected for a corner, and from it Charvet's header was held by Manninger on the line. When he cleared, Vialli obstructed him and was booked. Tempers and tantrums. But worse, Charvet's effort was to prove Chelsea's only on-target threat all game.

Arsenal extended their lead four minutes before half-time and again Hughes was the scorer. Newton lost Anelka wide and fouled him. Bergkamp's free-kick found Adams losing Charvet, and Hughes was the first to react to his header across the six-yard box.

Gullit changed to 3–5–2 at half-time. This was the half-time that Graham Rix later claimed he had found Gullit banging his head hopelessly into his fist in the shower area as he tried to come up with a formation and selection, and had written down the beginnings of a side with only two defenders. In the end it was Granville who came on for Petrescu who was getting substituted more and more often. Immediately Chelsea looked more comfortable, more balanced. They never threatened to score, but the shape of their play gave them equal footing with Arsenal.

Wise got booked again and so did Bergkamp. 'We've just got to keep plodding on,' Wise despaired. 'Hopefully we'll get it right. We killed ourselves, gave a goal away after four minutes. We had a plan set, what to do, and it went out the window.'

Chelsea missed another opportunity to close in on the leaders. Worst of all, Arsenal moved to a point behind Chelsea with a game in hand. For the first time in a season of 'bubbling under' for them, they were beginning to look like possible title challengers.

	Arsenal	Chelsea
Shots on target	3	1
Corners	4	4
Fouls	19	16
Offsides	5	1
Bookings	3	4

Bould on Vialli (12), Parlour, encroachment (13); Bergkamp on Wise (90); Vialli, foul (14), Leboeuf, foul (26), Wise, foul (63), Di Matteo, foul (66).

It's my second year, we're still in second place. Chelsea is still doing a good job.

Ruud Gullit

	Arsenal	Chelsea
Goals	2	0
S Hughes (4, 41)		

From Gullit to Vialli

THE SHOCK OF THE SEASON

When the sacking of Ruud Gullit was announced to the world on the afternoon of 12 February 1998, with Gianluca Vialli taking over immediately, there was virtually no-one who wasn't gobsmacked.

It emerged that on the Monday managing director Colin Hutchinson had approached Vialli about the possibility of becoming player-manager, and that on Wednesday evening they had agreed a deal.

Meanwhile, on Wednesday, Hutchinson had been meeting with Rangers' Brian Laudrup in a bid to secure his signature for next season. Gullit had him and PSV Eindhoven defender Stam at the top of his list. Vialli had also met Laudrup, but as a player who had moved into central London from another country, not as potential player-manager.

I got my first clue of what was to happen on that Wednesday evening but didn't register it. A mole telephoned me to say there would be a press conference the following evening. The suggestion was that Chelsea were signing Patrick Kluivert from Milan. I knew this to be unlikely.

When assistant manager Gwyn Williams telephoned later on his way back from a youth match I put the press conference

rumour to him, but he killed it.

Next day Hutchinson was at the training ground, and he suggested that I ought to go to Stamford Bridge in the afternoon. It was while I was driving through the gates that the radio told me the news. I was stunned.

Hutchinson had told Gullit immediately after training of the decision, and Gullit had stormed off in search of chairman Ken Bates. He thus missed the second piece of news, that his successor was to be Gianluca Vialli.

He believed that Hutchinson, Vialli and Williams had prepared the move behind his back, and would not speak to Williams after the events. But Williams, like just about everyone else, was ignorant of what was going on.

During the following weekend I telephoned Ruud in Amsterdam. I just wanted to wish him all the best and thank him for his co-operation in the work we did. He was completely baffled by his sacking.

There was, I suggested, a complete cultural divide between his laid-back attitude, his distaste for slog, his disinterest in traditional management activities, and what the club expected. 'But what do they want?' he demanded. 'What business is it of theirs what I do? They wanted results and I gave them to them. They wanted entertainment and I gave them that.'

And he did. But nothing in life is simple, and nothing concerning Ruud is simple either.

Ruud had held a press conference on the Friday when he insisted there was a hidden agenda to get rid of him. It can't have been just the money as Chelsea claimed. That led to the famous retort of Colin Hutchinson on *Clubcall* when he pointed out that Ruud's claim that he asked for two million pounds a year was in fact: 'Netto. I always talk netto.' In other words, he was demanding, before tax, well over three million pounds a year.

Chelsea were second, in contention for the Championship, in the last eight of the European Cup Winners' Cup and hanging on in the last four of the Coca-Cola Cup. They were in their best all-round position since 1965 when Tommy Docherty was in charge. So how can you sack the manager?

But experience is an invaluable asset, and Chelsea had plenty of experience of snatching defeat from the lap of victory. They didn't want to do it again.

Ian Porterfield took Chelsea to fourth at Christmas and the quarter-finals of the Coca-Cola Cup before sinking to twelve games without a win and towards lower table worries. Glenn Hoddle revolutionized Chelsea, kept failing to sign his new contract, and left in the final week of the season to manage England. Chelsea wanted security. Ruud wasn't working hard, wasn't fulfilling his job

Chelsea. The successes were his. He didn't mix much with anyone at the club. His life was his own. He didn't bother with analysing his decisions because he didn't need to. He just won.

But when things started going wrong, there was no foundation to help make them go right. There was no-one to talk to. There wasn't a method of analysis. There wasn't an open relationship with the players.

On the surface he didn't seem concerned and kept working in the same way. But he was concerned. He used to say he didn't watch football videos at home as part of his work, but I could often hear football in the background when I spoke with him on the telephone. Maybe his image-building did him an injustice.

The taking off of Mondays to do his coaching course didn't help, and one week when he moved the players' day off from Wednesday to Tuesday so that he could do some non-Chelsea work didn't make too many friends either.

Worse still was his diplomacy. One day when chairman Ken Bates dropped in to the training ground and hung around for half an hour swapping pleasantries in the canteen, he requested two minutes with Ruud in private. 'Nah,' responded Ruud, jumping up, 'I have to go to the bank.' And he walked out.

But he didn't care. He provided success and entertainment and that was the bottom line.

Perhaps the most surprising thing was that Ruud Gullit was such a superstar and yet he had been upstaged.

He will go down as one of Chelsea's great managers and, surely, as their greatest player. His influence was enormous. He will also go down as the man who benefited from Glenn Hoddle's revolutionary reign, without which Ruud's laid-back approach would surely not have been enough. But equally likely is that Glenn would not have been so successful had he not been able to bring Ruud's swagger to the team's play.

definition as a player, the team had lost its way over the last two months, work towards new signings was being handicapped by his own refusal to commit to the club, and the last straw was probably the Coca-Cola Cup defeat and his playing part in it at Highbury.

My own witnessing of Ruud Gullit's reign goes as follows.

The man was a genius. He was a superstar too, which was fantastic for image and publicity. But he didn't have to try and that was his downfall.

He brought to management what he had practiced as a player. He saw pictures, he made decisions. He didn't work at it. He decided which player to sign, he didn't even see them sometimes, and it worked. He decided which tactics to follow and it worked. He watched games and saw the picture and made his decision and it was usually right.

He didn't discuss it with others at

> *Ruudi has been wonderful for Chelsea. He may not believe it now, but we are very, very grateful for what he has brought us. But we have done the right thing for Chelsea Football Club, and I believe Gianluca Vialli can be a great Chelsea manager.*
>
> **Colin Hutchinson**

Vialli is more of a worker than Gullit, but less of a genius. He was respected by the players for who he was as well as what he was. But he was also a superstar, also a serial winner. And unlike Ruud he was willing to agree to a contract that would take in the period when he stopped being a full-time player and therefore earned less.

He was loved by the crowd. But he had to be a winner. And a winner with bundles of style. The supporters would settle for nothing less because that was what Ruud Gullit had given them until very near the end.

Wednesday 18 February
Stamford Bridge
34,430

Chelsea 3 Arsenal 1

CHELSEA WON 4–3 ON AGGREGATE

What a start for Gianluca Vialli. Qualification for Wembley! Would the team have come back like this under Ruud Gullit? Had Chelsea's board pulled off their own stroke of genius?

Extraordinarily, the home supporters hardly gave a whisper of discontent over the Gullit decision. They got behind Vialli from the moment he appeared.

Was it the occasion? Was it the man, apparently so harshly treated by Gullit? Or was it perhaps the two million pounds 'netto' revelation that had given a clear indication that Gullit was misleading the public.

Vialli kept his team and formation under wraps. He wanted it to be a surprise for Arsenal. There was so much at stake – not just his relationship with a post-Gullit crowd, but now a European place. UEFA had confirmed they were giving way in their fight with the Football League, so the Coca-Cola winners would qualify for the UEFA Cup.

Rumours in the media that Chelsea would play 4–3–3 with Zola tucked in behind Vialli and another striker were wrong. He wanted 4–3–3 with one central striker and two wide from the outset. And in time he wanted to introduce this throughout the club.

Arsenal had problems. Internationals Seaman, Keown, Bould and Wright were injured, but they chose to leave Stephen Hughes, curse of Chelsea, on the bench. Chelsea were without Sinclair who had returned from international duty with Jamaica suffering from a calf strain.

Can you imagine the atmosphere? Arsenal fans had the whole of the uncovered West Stand lower tier the length of the pitch. It was fearsome.

From the off it was clear there were changes. 'They played only long balls and pressured on the second ball,' remarked Arsenal manager Wenger with surprise. And he added carefully: 'I think everybody was a little more concentrated. They were the very offensive team and defended hard and I don't think that can last.'

Coach Graham Rix was quick to point out that there is a difference between launching long balls forward and passing the

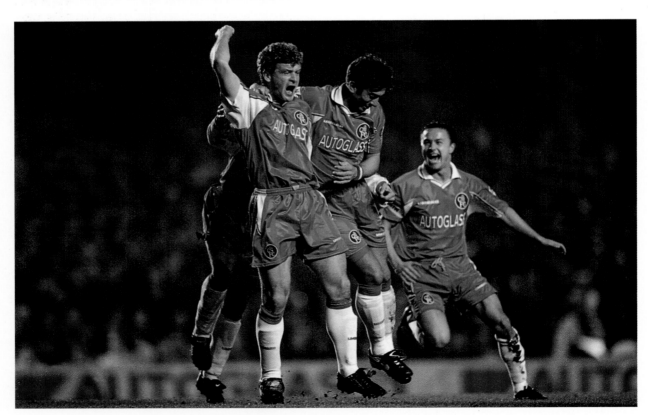

Mark Hughes celebrates making the aggregate scores level

Chelsea

de Goey

Clarke   Duberry   Leboeuf   Le Saux

Petrescu   Wise   Di Matteo

Zola   M Hughes   Vialli
(Newton 80)

Referee: **Graham Poll** (Tring, Herts)

Anelka   Bergkamp

Overmars   Petit   Vieira   Parlour
(Platt 45)

Winterburn   Adams   Grimandi   Dixon
(S Hughes 70)

Manninger

Arsenal

ball quickly and long to the front players, and that was what Chelsea were doing.

Other things, however, did not change. Hughes was booked for kicking out at Vieira after three minutes and Dixon for a high challenge on Zola after eight.

One minute later Chelsea took the lead. It had to be Hughes. Three-quarters of the ground went wild. Zola's corner was headed out by Parlour, and when Di Matteo dribbled back into the penalty area the ball ran to Hughes who swivelled and thumped it low between a clutch of defenders just inside the post on the blind side of the way he had turned. Pandemonium!

The first-half became a battle to equal the atmosphere. Arsenal needed an away goal not just to retake the lead but to put pressure on Chelsea for the rest of the tie. There was only one good effort though, and that was Chelsea's, but Zola's twenty-five-yarder flew fractionally over.

Zola worked hard off the right flank but often looked too far from the danger zone. A quarter of an hour before half-time Vialli turned up on that side and cleverly won a corner. His confidence inflated wonderfully, and he immediately started turning all his hard work into penetrating damage for Arsenal.

But what a battle it was. Chelsea suffered one more booking and Arsenal three before the interval. And two minutes into the second-half Vieira, one of those first-half naughty boys when he tripped Vialli, tripped Le Saux and was sent off.

Chelsea immediately sewed up the tie. Di Matteo latched onto a loose ball just inside Arsenal's half after Hughes had massacred Platt, raced forward thirty yards and hit an unbelievable high riser thirty more yards into Manninger's top corner. Di Matteo was clearly a player for big games.

Two minutes later Petrescu controlled a header out from Zola's corner, jinked inside Adams and Petit and placed a sidefooter carefully into the gap at the far post.

On the hour Dixon managed Arsenal's first shot, but it was wild. More bookings followed, including Wise for a foul on Bergkamp. With ten minutes to go Duberry handled when on the floor and Bergkamp put away the penalty. Another Arsenal goal would win them the tie on away goals if the aggregate was a draw. Both sets of supporters screamed their all. It was brilliant.

But Chelsea came nearest to scoring again, one minute from time when Zola, after a one-two with Di Matteo, forced Manninger to turn his shot round.

Afterwards Di Matteo, typically, was the gentleman. 'We're all happy for our new manager, we have still in mind the old manager and we thank him for everything he did for us. A bit of this victory is also his.'

So too was Zola. 'When you are supported by a team that is very solid behind you don't have any problems. We were very solid and it allowed us to play completely free.'

Chelsea back at Wembley. What a year this was going to be.

	Chelsea	Arsenal
Shots on target	5	1
Corners	4	10
Fouls	23	22
Offsides	7	5
Bookings	4	4

Hughes, foul (3), Clarke, foul (27), Duberry, foul (55), Wise, foul (76); Dixon on Zola (8), Parlour on Wise (29), Adams on Di Matteo (39), Petit on Vialli (74).

Sending off	0	1

Vieira, two bookings, on Vialli (37) and Le Saux (47)

> ❛The players were fantastic. We changed the organization of the team. It was a game we had to win by working hard on the pitch. I couldn't expect better from the players. The pressure before the match was huge. Sometimes you think that football is just a game but it's very difficult to handle it.❜
>
> Gianluca Vialli

	Chelsea	Arsenal
Goals	3	1

M Hughes (9), Di Matteo (50), Petrescu (52); Bergkamp (pen) (81)

Saturday 21 February
Filbert Street
21,335

Leicester City 2 Chelsea 0

FOURTH PREMIERSHIP AWAY DEFEAT IN SUCCESSION

How many times in Chelsea's history has the problem of inconsistency been debated? In 1997 as Chelsea battled to finish in a UEFA Cup qualifying position for the first time since 1971, League form died as FA Cup progress built up.

By the time of the quarter-finals, League games had become secondary. A UEFA Cup place was missed by one position. It was just as well that Chelsea won the Cup.

Now a UEFA Cup spot was one Coca-Cola Cup victory away. But if Chelsea lost, the League position would become vital. After the investment of the summer and the ousting of Gullit, European qualification was crucial for the club just to stand still, never mind develop.

But try telling that to the players on a Saturday afternoon at Filbert Street, drained by the emotions of the last ten days and the immensity of Wednesday's win. Leicester were big and strong and since promotion a season before had never beaten Chelsea in League or Cup, twice losing to late goals.

With de Goey away on international duty, Kharine started his first game in eighteen months. He had eight reserve appearances behind him, but after so long out with such a debilitating injury it would have been unrealistic to expect the world class performer with thirty-six Russian caps to be in top form. What he needed was time and games.

However, he was allowed no time. Leicester were gifted the lead after two minutes. As Le Saux was leaping to head out an inswinging corner, Leicester's Heskey ran from far post to near. His marker, Leboeuf, pushed out to play offside, but when former Chelsea midfielder Izzet headed the ball back into the area unchallenged by the nearby Zola, Heskey was onside and unmarked six yards out. He beat Kharine without fuss.

You could argue all day about whose fault it was, whether it was lack of marking or lack of organization. But it was certainly lack of concentration.

As the minutes wore on Chelsea got frustrated and finished up collecting bookings. Wise, of course, was the first, for a two-footed tackle.

Midfielder Lennon gets to grips with Di Matteo

Leicester

Arphexad

Prior   Elliott   Kaamark
(Campbell 80)

Savage   Lennon   Zagorakis   Izzet   Guppy
(Walsh 24)

Cottee   Heskey
(Fenton 45)

Referee: **Paul Durkin** (Portland, Dorset)

Zola   M Hughes   Vialli
(Flo 71)

Di Matteo   Wise   Petrescu

Le Saux   Leboeuf   Duberry   Clarke

Kharine

Chelsea

Every opposition home crowd wanted the scalp of Chelsea, the flash foreigners, the dilettante entertainers, and in small grounds like Leicester's the atmosphere was very hostile. Leicester weren't very good but they were hard, and the battle wore on to draining effect.

Just before half-time Wise's thirty-yarder took Arphexad two attempts to hold the ball and just after the hour Leboeuf's thirty-yard free-kick was brilliantly – if flashily – caught by Arphexad. The 4–3–3 formation didn't seem to suit the team particularly well. Outnumbered in midfield and too often marooned in attack, there was no rhythm or pattern to Chelsea's play, just battle.

Kharine lacked confidence whenever the ball was crossed low into the box.

Duberry heads off Heskey

Later he confided he was surprised by how often and how hard low fiercely-hit crosses were blazed into the area – a change in general tactics from eighteen months ago. Leicester created and missed two chances from such balls just after Flo had come on for a weary Zola.

With eight minutes left Chelsea managed an effort from inside the penalty area for the first time. Le Saux's header from Petrescu's cross brought a terrific reflex save from Arphexad.

In the circumstances a draw would have been a good result for Chelsea, and that attempt nearly brought one. Rix had moved personnel round midway through the second-half: Clarke to left-back, Le Saux to left midfield, Di Matteo to right midfield and Petrescu to right-back. The wide men moved clockwise but nothing much improved.

Two minutes from time Heskey scored his second goal and his fifth of the season. What a mess it was. Duberry lost possession, Leboeuf won it back off Izzet, the ball broke loose but Petrescu lost out in a tackle with Guppy, the ball running loose to Duberry who kicked it against the fallen Izzet. Heskey then flicked it to Guppy before running into space for a low return cross which foxed Kharine and left Heskey with a two-yard tap-in.

Suddenly Chelsea were eleven points behind the leaders and down to fourth place. For the first time since the season had got healthily underway Arsenal overtook them as they accelerated into second place. Never mind the Championship, it was time to muscle out some points if a UEFA Cup place was to be obtained. But could this Chelsea team do that?

Questions about their long-term effectiveness were now being asked more and more frequently.

> *We lost the match in that first twenty minutes. We are still in a sort of limbo. We are still one of the best teams in the Premier League, but unfortunately we are not the best one yet. I think we can improve. I'm not too worried about this defeat because I think it has come from the great effort of the tiring game we had on Wednesday.*
>
> Gianluca Vialli

	Leicester	Chelsea
Shots on target	2	5
Corners	6	5
Fouls	7	10
Offsides	9	8
Bookings	2	3

Lennon, dissent (30), Izzet, shooting after the whistle had blown(39); Wise, foul (19); Di Matteo, foul (29); M Hughes, dissent (40).

	Leicester	Chelsea
Goals	2	0

Heskey (2, 88)

Saturday 28 February
Stamford Bridge
34,511

Chelsea 0 Manchester United 1

THE END OF THE PREMIERSHIP DREAM

One year ago, on 22 February, on the back of a magnificent Christmas and New Year, Chelsea had fought themselves into Premiership contention. Now, following a magnificent start to the season spoilt by an appalling Christmas and New Year, they were clinging on to it.

A year ago they were twelve points behind leaders Manchester United with two games in hand when United came to Stamford Bridge. If they had beaten United and won those two games they would have been just three points behind. Now, they were eleven points behind with one game in hand. The two wins would leave them still five points behind. So after all the glorious football of autumn, Chelsea were worse off than a year ago.

Back then, their form was awesome. In the first-half they pulverized United, Zola scored an outrageous individual goal after two minutes, and all was well with the world. But in the second-half fatigue crept in, not helped by a prestigious friendly away to AC Milan three days before, and United equalized. The Premiership dream drifted away.

This time, there had been no midweek interference apart from international call-ups on both sides. Under the new Vialli regime training was already a lot tougher than under Gullit. Tuesday's requirements had involved a morning and afternoon session followed by the senior players being called in for a meeting with Vialli. At 5pm Graham Rix turned to Eddie Newton and laughed:

Midfielder Butt makes a fist of controlling Wise

Chelsea

Kharine

Clarke Duberry Leboeuf Le Saux

Petrescu Wise Di Matteo

Vialli M Hughes Zola
(Flo 78)

*Referee: **Steve Dunn** (Bristol)*

Cole Sheringham

Butt Scholes P Neville Beckham

Irwin Pallister Johnsen G Neville
(Berg 27)

Schmeichel

Manchester United

'You haven't worked this late since you were on YTS!'

United had injury problems going into the game but got everybody except Giggs ready. Surprisingly, they played Butt wide on the left and Phil Neville in central midfield. Before the half hour they lost Pallister to a back injury but they were able to cope with their problems.

On the half hour they scored the only goal of the game as Phil Neville ran unmarked onto Sheringham's chip over Leboeuf before placing it across a stranded Kharine and in off the post. It was the first goal of his career.

Nine minutes later, Petrescu's twenty-five-yarder on the back of a forty-yard sprint, athletically turned over by Schmeichel, was Chelsea's only test of the goalkeeper all game.

The day just never took off for Chelsea. An 11.15am kick-off to co-operate with television and preparations for the return of both teams to Europe in midweek led to a quiet crowd. The skill and flair of earlier in the season seemed to be lost in the hard work required of the three-man midfield, and the strength required just didn't materialize.

There were some good moments early on. Gary Neville cleared a Petrescu cross from the six-yard box and Scholes got in crucial blocks on Di Matteo and Petrescu. But United had a stranglehold on affairs and nothing much happened. A quiet game couldn't fire up a capacity crowd.

Just before United scored you could sense that they were stepping up a gear and Kharine was quick off his line to block from Cole, his best save since his return. But after the goal the frustrations tumbled out and the old edginess crept in. Bookings began to be picked up, including an angry Wise who collected his eleventh of the season, and thus faced a third suspension and a trip to the FA Disciplinary Committee.

Chelsea fought on in the second-half, enjoying more possession, but never got near a breakthrough.

United manager Alex Ferguson was delighted. 'We recognize that Chelsea are challengers. They have made strides over the last two or three years. That's why today's game and result for us was very important. I thought Chelsea were our main challengers this year. I think this result makes it very difficult for them now.'

It seemed as if United had more knowhow. Petrescu admitted: 'Their defence is the best in England, maybe in Europe. We had some chances but we have to be more solid. At the end of the day it was a very professional job by them. They created one or two chances and that was the difference.'

So far, Vialli had brilliantly turned round a Cup tie but had not rescued League form. Chelsea dropped to fifth, fourteen points behind United and three behind Arsenal who had a game in hand. The worst thing about these stumbling performances was the scarcity of goalscoring chances. Suddenly this fantastic free-scoring side didn't look capable of hitting the net. In his post-match press conference Vialli conceded that the title dream was over.

But the season wasn't.

> *The new system, you have to work hard and we did. We seemed to have stopped teams creating chances, they didn't have a clear-cut one in the second-half, but we've got to get back to how we were at the other end.*
>
> **Michael Duberry**

	Chelsea	Man Utd
Shots on target	1	2
Corners	10	1
Fouls	17	15
Offsides	4	3
Bookings	3	3

Wise, foul (43), Zola, foul (50), Leboeuf, foul (83); Butt on Wise (33), Beckham, dissent (43), Cole on Clarke (65).

	Chelsea	Man Utd
Goals	0	1

P Neville (30)

Thursday 5 March
Benito Villamarin Stadium
23,018

Real Betis 1 Chelsea 2

SUDDENLY, THE BEST PERFORMANCE OF THE SEASON

Chelsea and Stuttgart had been favourites to win the European Cup Winners' Cup from the beginning, and when the quarter-final draw was made in Geneva just before Christmas the Stuttgart delegate had told Chelsea's Colin Hutchinson that the Blues were the one team they didn't want to meet.

But since Christmas both sides had suffered a serious dip in form while Spain's Real Betis had gone bombing up their table and were now in serious contention with Real Madrid for second spot and a European Champions' League place behind Barcelona.

Betis had become one of the most commercially successful clubs in Spain, mirroring Chelsea's progress in England, and the tie was clearly the biggest of the round.

Relations between the clubs got off to a bad footing as Betis wanted to give Chelsea fewer than 500 tickets. After UEFA arbitrated the total was advanced to 1500 but they were all terrace tickets. Betis then further infuriated Chelsea by selling tickets to unofficial independent travelling supporters in the section of the ground right next to the official party.

Worse still, the official party had to be in the stadium three hours before kick-off. There were no facilities and no floodlights and the rain poured down.

Betis had some excellent players, not least the Croatian captain and left-winger Jarni and Spain's centre-forward Alfonso. But as a club they lacked European experience, and this was the biggest night of their lives.

They froze. Chelsea won the tactical game, and although a lot of reports afterwards claimed they were lucky to hold on to their lead, that was rubbish. Chelsea were robbed of two further goals by bad officiating.

That was an irony as the originally selected officials had to be changed after being spotted at Betis' League match the weekend before the tie. The new referee was familiar as he had taken charge of Chelsea's home leg with Austria Memphis in 1994.

Vialli changed his tactics for the first time. He stuck to a variation of 4–3–3, but it was a big variation. Really it was 4–3–2–1, and Betis never coped. He told his three midfielders, Newton, Wise and Di Matteo, to stay tight and compact, and he told Petrescu and Zola to play free from right and left, but essentially to be two further midfielders. In effect, Petrescu drifted back into midfield and Zola up into attack, half making Chelsea 4–4–2, but when the midfield needed bolstering Chelsea always had an extra man there.

Le Saux and Granville had both picked up injuries during the week, so Sinclair was rushed back with virtually no training to play

Prats parted his legs and Flo shot through

Prats

Solozabal   **Vidakovic**   **Olias**
(Marquez 45)

Cañas   **Alexis**   **Merino**   **Fernando**
(Oli 65)

George   **Jarni**

Alfonso

Real Betis

*Referee: **Atanas Ouzounov** (Bulgaria)*

Flo
(M Hughes 84)

Zola   **Petrescu**
(Nicholls 78)

Di Matteo   **Wise**   **Newton**

Sinclair   **Leboeuf**   **Duberry**   **Clarke**

de Goey

Chelsea

at left-back.

Vialli also surprised everyone by leaving out Mark Hughes and himself and adding an extra midfielder, the battling Newton.

Flo, with his pace and strength, was just the man to play alone up front. It was a role he played for Norway, and on this night he played himself into Chelsea fans' hearts. By the final whistle they were singing his name. Vialli had pulled off his first tactical coup.

Seven minutes had gone when Flo took Di Matteo's fine pass up the right, turned the unimpressive Olias and raced twenty yards into the penalty area where he checked as sweeper Vidakovic challenged and then went outside him before cutting in and sending a low searing shot beyond Prats and just inside the far post. What a goal! It was right in front of the Chelsea fans too.

Four minutes later the lanky Norwegian repeated the process after Clarke had won the ball off Jarni. This time Petrescu fed him. He went outside Olias but in the area, after checking, turned inside Vidakovic and blasted the ball through Prats' legs.

Betis were good going forward but Chelsea defended superbly. Leboeuf's covering tackle on Cañas on the quarter hour after racing across the area was surely the tackle of the season. De Goey dealt with all Jarni's fierce inswinging corners, punching with authority, and athletically turned over Fernando's strongly lobbed header from a long cross.

Just before half-time Zola tricked his way past Betis' best defender, Solozabal, went past Vidakovic in the box and was dragged down. Incredibly, the referee booked Zola for diving. Chelsea should have had a penalty and gone in at half-

time 3–0 up. As it was Vidakovic limped off with a hamstring tear and didn't play in the second leg. Then the big and strong Fernando was booked for hacking down Petrescu and that put him out of the second leg too.

Betis substitute Marquez lined up at right wing-back with their team shuffling round, and he was excellent. Immediately he turned Sinclair before delivering a cross right onto Alfonso's head. The goal put Betis back in the tie. But then the Spaniard missed an easy header from eight yards and sent another from close range straight at de Goey. At the other end Sinclair was high with a free header from one Zola corner and had another cleared off the line from a second. But most infuriating was the disallowing of Petrescu's excellent goal after he had burst through and fallen prey to the linesman's wrongly raised flag. That should have made it 4–1.

The game grew open. Wise, Duberry and substitute Nicholls were booked, bringing pressure for the rest of the competition. De Goey stretched with superb reactions to fist away Jarni's swerving thirty-five-yard free-kick and reacted well to the same player's close-range header. But Chelsea continued to create, and Prats dashed ten yards beyond his area to tackle Petrescu and later punched the air in relief when his miskick finished up with substitute Mark Hughes miskicking as well.

Marquez continued to send in dangerous crosses and in the last three minutes Jarni and the Nigerian international Finidi George left an inviting ball to each other and Alfonso's header from a Finidi cross was pushed away by de Goey.

Chelsea had enjoyed the benefit of a perfect playing surface. Betis stuck to their formation throughout, moving Alfonso back when big Oli came on. They were good at playing their way. But they weren't good enough as Chelsea played with the flair of earlier in the season.

	Real Betis	Chelsea
Shots on target	7	3
Corners	11	2
Fouls	9	18
Offsides	5	5
Bookings	4	3

Fernando on Petrescu (44), Solozabal on Flo (65), Jarni on Wise(76); Zola, dive (41), Wise, handball (61), Duberry, kicking ball away after whistle had blown (77), Nicholls, foul (78).

❝ *I think in the first-half we played brilliant football. In the second-half in the first minute they make it 1–2, and then we get some problems. But after fifteen minutes we are having the control back and we have to score more goals. That is the only thing we are missing.* ❞

Ed de Goey

	Real Betis	Chelsea
Goals	1	2

Alfonso (46); Flo (7, 11)

Sunday 8 March
Stamford Bridge
33,018

Chelsea 0 Aston Villa 1
FOURTH CONSECUTIVE SCORELESS PREMIERSHIP DEFEAT

Chelsea were in the Coca-Cola Cup Final and half-way to the European Cup Winners' Cup semi-final. But where was the next Premiership goal going to come from? And what about the crowd? There was lack of focus there, certainly. For the first time in the League the gate was over a thousand down on capacity. An expensive Cup Final plus attractive overseas games were taking their financial toll. The League was losing importance.

Villa had a different kind of focus. They too had played in Spain in midweek, on Tuesday in the UEFA Cup. They lost 1–0 to Atletico Madrid who were below Real Betis in the table, yet mysteriously

Vialli, on taking over from Gullit, had expressed the wish to pick his best team every game, but was finding it impossible. 'We are playing so many matches in a short time. I would like to play the same team or best possible team but I have to consider someone needs a rest.' Clarke, Petrescu, Wise and Zola were rested. Hughes was suspended. Myers, who missed Spain because of the protracted birth of his first son, played without having had much sleep.

The 4–3–3 formation didn't help, as Vialli recognized. 'The system is quite tiring. It is not easy, especially when you change

Leboeuf heads away from Yorke but Chelsea head to another defeat

Villa got a better press than Chelsea, something that rankled with many fans. Manchester United also got a better press after their 0–0 draw in Monaco on Wednesday. Chelsea's winning achievement was put down to luck. We would see.

Villa had a further problem besides their European defeat. They were battling away from relegation under new manager John Gregory and they urgently needed points.

something in February, you need time to settle.'

He knew the system depended on hard work, closing the opposition down early, pressurizing them, winning the ball early, and playing from there. It depended also on getting the ball forward early. You had to be fit.

With Coca-Cola and European progress, fatigue was becoming a major factor.

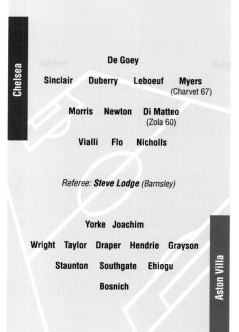

Chelsea

De Goey

Sinclair Duberry Leboeuf Myers
(Charvet 67)

Morris Newton Di Matteo
(Zola 60)

Vialli Flo Nicholls

Referee: **Steve Lodge** (Barnsley)

Yorke Joachim

Wright Taylor Draper Hendrie Grayson

Staunton Southgate Ehiogu

Bosnich

Aston Villa

The game started wonderfully for Eddie Newton and ended seriously badly for Zola. Homegrown midfielder Newton captained the team for the first time. 'I'm very proud to have led Chelsea out,' he said afterwards, and there was no doubting he was.

But from the start Chelsea were again disjointed and lacked the pace and strength to infiltrate the opposition penalty area. Nicholls, like Zola, lacked the pace and strength to work from wide. Morris, coming into midfield, lacked games and needed to work on his fitness. He was also out of form in the reserves and failed to produce anything penetrating here.

Villa were solid but undynamic. They paired Joachim with Yorke up front because the expensive Collymore and the unpopular Milosevic were injured. Their team seemed a better unit than earlier in the season.

Vialli had a couple of early efforts, shooting wide from Flo's back-flick and chipping over after Morris had done well to transfer Leboeuf's crossfield pass quickly to Sinclair.

Towards half-time Nicholls had a couple of chances, but was blocked by Ehiogu after Bosnich's punch had failed to gain distance and was then blocked by the goalkeeper after a defensive mix-up. Chelsea weren't creating so much as huffing and puffing and Villa were making mistakes.

It was a pretty even game in front of another unimpassioned crowd. Grayson got past Di Matteo and Myers but his average cross produced a poor header; Wright's wicked cross was crucially cleared by Duberry; de Goey saved Joachim's header and watched Taylor shoot over.

Neither side was useless, but neither was ever more than useful. Here was a

game to be won by a focused side, however tired of limb.

Villa won it five minutes into the second-half. Duberry had already painfully blocked Taylor's bombshell with his face when Morris' tackle failed to stop the influential Draper dribbling across the face of the eighteen-yard line. He forced the ball through to a depressingly unmarked Joachim who had time to turn and fire across de Goey.

'We're always chasing the game,' complained Rix. 'We were chasing the game against Villa, we were chasing the game against United. It's interesting that we scored early in Betis and it seemed to give us heart.'

Vialli showed the frustration of the management when after losing the ball and not winning the free-kick he wanted he raced to Hendrie and pinched his cheek while giving a fiery lecture. He was lucky to stay on the pitch.

Chelsea's whole game perked up when Zola came on after an hour. He seemed refreshed. He whipped in an acute angled free-kick which Bosnich turned over. He whipped a corner in for a free Leboeuf header which went over. His great skills took him past Ehiogu and his cross for Vialli was well turned away by Staunton for another corner. At least Chelsea were finishing strongly.

De Goey had to save well from Joachim before, with two minutes to go, an excellent run by Flo set up Zola alone in the inside-left position in the penalty area. The great Italian had not scored for three months since his hat-trick against Derby on 29 November. Suddenly his whole sapping drought seemed to rear up inside him and destroy the confidence he had paraded for half an hour. He drew back his left foot and wimpishly sliced the ball wide of the goal. Head in hands, he turned and ran back to start again. But it was too late.

Chelsea had problems, for sure, but Zola was developing the biggest problems of all.

	Chelsea	Aston Villa
Shots on target	1	4
Corners	6	6
Fouls	8	10
Offsides	1	10
Bookings	1	1

Vialli, attacking player (83); Staunton, dissent (79).

> ❝ *I don't think we were poor, but we were tired. We've got to learn what Man United do. It is hard going. You've got to be mentally tuned in, you come from the high of Real Betis and it is hard. It's hard to step in and perform as well. Mentally when you need that half a yard it sometimes isn't there, and you could see that today.* ❞
>
> **Eddie Newton**

	Chelsea	Aston Villa
Goals	0	1

Joachim (50)

Wednesday 11 March
Stamford Bridge
31,917

Chelsea 6 Crystal Palace 2

FOURTH SIX-GOAL HAUL OF THE SEASON

Something needed doing. The players adored and respected Vialli but the new approach was working no better than the old one. The crowd dropped by over another thousand. This was a game originally postponed because of Palace's FA Cup progress but their League form was dire and they were bottom of the table.

Vialli decided to ditch 4–3–3. 'It's a very tiring system and you need all the players to be very fit and in good shape and that's not possible in this part of the season because we play so many matches in a short time. I talked to the players, and we decided together to play this system this evening, the same system they played. I thought we are better than them and if we play the same system there was no problem about organization.'

If it took strength to change his approach, it also took strength to make the announcement he chose to write in the programme. He wanted Kharine to have a chance to get match fit, and so he was going to play him in the remaining Premiership games. De Goey would play the Cup matches. De Goey wasn't happy, but he was playing so well and had joined Chelsea to win silverware, so for now he was keeping silent. Silverware wasn't far away.

With the chance to win two Cups it could yet turn into one of the best seasons in Chelsea's history. If only League form could be quickly turned round it could be turned into the best in Chelsea's history.

In the team talk before the game Rix turned over the sheets on his pad showing the various tactical requirements, and finished with a simple slogan on the last sheet: 'GIVE THE BALL TO ZOLA'.

Quickly someone added: 'And not to Dennis Wise.' Dressing room banter! Confidence grew.

Three things were immediately clear about the 3–5–2

Tore Andre Flo makes it six in the last minute

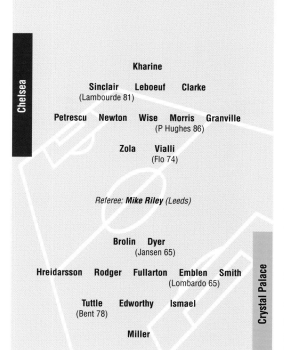

Chelsea

Kharine

Sinclair Leboeuf Clarke
(Lambourde 81)

Petrescu Newton Wise Morris Granville
(P Hughes 86)

Zola Vialli
(Flo 74)

Referee: Mike Riley (Leeds)

Brolin Dyer
(Jansen 65)

Hreidarsson Rodger Fullarton Emblen Smith
(Lombardo 65)

Tuttle Edworthy Ismael
(Bent 78)

Miller

Crystal Palace

formation. It suited sweeper Leboeuf and wing-back Petrescu. It suited Zola who seemed to get the ball ten to twenty yards further forward where he could do more damage. And it was the only formation in which Chelsea had won in the Premiership this year.

However, the game started with a hiccup when Hreidarsson hit a sizzling low twenty-yarder into the far corner, Chelsea having failed to clear in a mêlée after Kharine had punched out a long ball. Then the fun started.

Goal 1: Vialli poked home after Sinclair had headed down Zola's corner.

Goal 2: Zola ended his bad run and fell to his knees in front of the Shed Umbro Stand. He had received the ball on the right from Newton after Vialli had won it in the Chelsea half and pushed it to Wise who had zig-zagged past two challenges. Zola knocked it into Vialli in the centre of play, and then surged into the area where Vialli passed for him to tuck it past Tuttle, round Miller and touch it in. Brilliant goal, brilliant player. Lay off Zola.

Goal 3: Zola's superb pass to Vialli after he had run his foot over the ball to bamboozle the defender gave the player-manager a clear shot. Miller blocked but Vialli turned skillfully to knock the ball back in from just inside the area.

Goal 4: Although it was 3–1 at half-time the fourth goal came with only seven minutes to go after Flo had replaced

Vialli. Chances had been missed. Then Petrescu and Flo combined to find Zola on the edge of the box. His perfect pass gave Wise the chance to step inside Brolin and choose his spot.

Hiccup: Substitute Bent raced onto substitute Lombardo's pass after substitute Paul Hughes had surrendered possession and easily beat Kharine one on one.

Goal 5: A minute later Flo bashed the ball through Miller after Petrescu had got wide from Hughes' pass and crossed low.

Goal 6: Two minutes later, in the last minute, Flo ran clear on to Hughes' pass and was lucky when Miller saved his shot that the ball rebounded into his path off Edworthy. He shot home from a tight angle. Flo had only been on sixteen minutes. How the Matthew Harding Stand sang his name.

Zola was back in immense form with the big Cup games coming up. The team looked in shape and created and scored goals. Wise was quick to praise his manager: 'Luca showed all the players what he wants and what he expects. He led by example. I thought he was magnificent.' Kharine and Morris both looked fitter. Duberry and Di Matteo had been rested. Fourth place in the Premiership was reclaimed.

But it wasn't all good. Palace were bottom and manager Steve Coppell was eased upstairs next day with Lombardo taking charge of team affairs. They were a team in a mess. All Chelsea had done was what they had been doing at the beginning of the season – annihilating the dregs of the Premiership. But at least they had done it.

> *In the past I've done very good games, high levels, but haven't been as consistent as last year. Today was very important to recovering my confidence, my skills, but now I need to make it a great game Saturday, then Thursday, then again Sunday. I would like to enjoy today but I have to be very tuned in.*
>
> **Gianfranco Zola**

	Chelsea	C Palace
Shots on target	13	5
Corners	3	5
Fouls	14	13
Offsides	1	12
Bookings	1	2

Granville, foul (80); Emblen on Vialli (25), Dyer, kicking ball after whistle had blown (43).

	Chelsea	C Palace
Goals	6	2

Vialli (14, 43), Zola (16), Wise (83), Flo (88, 90); Hreidarsson (6), Bent (87)

Assists

Vialli, Zola 2, Petrescu 2, P Hughes 2

Saturday 14 March
Boleyn Ground
25,829

West Ham United 2 Chelsea 1

FIFTH PREMIERSHIP AWAY DEFEAT IN SUCCESSION

Gianluca Vialli asked for two results in a row for the first time in his management. He made plenty of changes despite the 6–2 win on Wednesday. After all, Real Betis still had to be beaten on Thursday and this was Chelsea's fourth game in ten days.

Wise was suspended but Mark Hughes returned from suspension to captain the team. Zola, Clarke, Sinclair and Petrescu were rested. So Zola had to forego this opportunity to gain consistency. The 3–5–2 formation was retained, not so much because of its success on Wednesday but because it mirrored West Ham's formation, and once again Vialli felt Chelsea could win man for man.

West Ham were hoping for a UEFA Cup spot and so had plenty to play for. Chelsea had something to prove to themselves. And at the same time they had to prepare for Thursday. There was also the little fact that anyone sent off today for violent conduct would miss the Coca-Cola Final.

The Cup Final opponents Middlesbrough, beaten by Chelsea in last season's FA Cup Final, were undoubtedly a better team now than then, but there was absolutely no doubt in the Chelsea camp that if the Blues got their game right victory would be claimed. There was no doubt, either, that the Cup Winners' Cup was winnable.

Vialli had said before he had any idea that he would be Chelsea manager: 'As long as you can you have to keep your finger in all the pies.' How he loved English clichés. 'Because of our fitness, there is a lack of tiredness now. If you have the chance it is better to choose in April rather than January.' He was referring to focusing on one

Danny Granville heads away from Impey

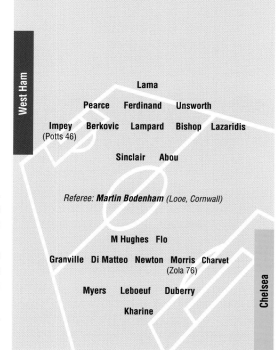

West Ham

Lama

Pearce　Ferdinand　Unsworth

Impey　Berkovic　Lampard　Bishop　Lazaridis
(Potts 46)

Sinclair　Abou

Referee: **Martin Bodenham** *(Looe, Cornwall)*

M Hughes　Flo

Granville　Di Matteo　Newton　Morris　Charvet
(Zola 76)

Myers　Leboeuf　Duberry

Kharine

Chelsea

competition in preference to another. He had been talking the week before Chelsea crashed out of the FA Cup to Manchester United.

Now, in March, with tired bodies everywhere the League seemed to be slipping behind the Cups in importance.

But it was so important to get a balance and a performance. Confidence was still vulnerable. In fairness, the balance was there against West Ham. Chelsea dragged their weary limbs through the first-half, never in too much danger of falling behind. It was a far from typical London derby with few fouls and few goalmouth incidents. The play was controlled but not aggressive. The capacity crowd sang and bantered but remained mostly calm.

For West Ham Ferdinand was outstanding at sweeper, but they too lacked any other special presence.

Six minutes into the second-half, just after Di Matteo had crashed a left footer closely over, he took a wide free-kick following a foul on Flo. Charvet, starting a game for only the second time, got away from Lampard to head powerfully into the top corner. He may not have spoken English but he knew how to celebrate with his team-mates.

Suddenly, Chelsea had the chance to claim the classic away victory of a successful team. Like Manchester United at Stamford Bridge two weeks ago, defend, strangle, use your energy sensibly, strike when you have the chance, then kill the game. The marathon experts' away win.

Instead, the Blues caved in. A quarter of an hour of little action later, substitute Potts was allowed to burst forward from the back, and for goodness knows how many times

in the season, the defence pushed forward but failed to organize its offside act, and Trevor Sinclair raced through to equalize.

Six minutes later there was mayhem following a corner, just like at Leicester. Kharine punched out, Di Matteo let Bishop get past him on the edge of the area and shoot, Morris stretched to knock the ball away but it fell to the unmarked Unsworth who finished at the near post. It was dreadful defending.

Chelsea sent on Zola to try and add spark but played him in midfield where he hardly touched the ball. What a waste!

So, instead of a classic performance it was an infuriating one. There were few efforts on goal again, and their was a lack of cutting edge about the side.

Flo and Hughes failed to spark each other and Duberry still lacked sharpness. Kharine and Morris both needed more time if they were to prove they could get back to their best. Charvet was neat but apart from his goal a peripheral figure. The players had played as a team, but the individuals had not looked special.

Rix was disappointed. 'We want to finish as high as possible. There were players out there to a certain extent who were playing for their places on Thursday.'

Away form was simply not good enough. And to prove it, Leeds and Blackburn now had the same number of points as Chelsea, Blackburn with a game in hand, and Derby moved to within three points, also with a game in hand. Derby was the next away game. It could all end in disaster.

But Chelsea could be well on the way to glory before Derby were visited.

	West Ham	Chelsea
Shots on target	5	3
Corners	6	3
Fouls	6	9
Offsides	6	3
Bookings	1	2

Unsworth on Flo (69); Charvet, foul (20), Newton, dissent (80).

'*It was a reasonable performance first-half and once we got our noses in front we should have seen it out. There was nothing wrong with the team play, but we just couldn't keep our lead.*'

Mark Hughes

	West Ham	Chelsea
Goals	2	1

Sinclair (67), Unsworth (73); Charvet (51)

Assist
Di Matteo

Thursday 19 March
Stamford Bridge
32,300

Chelsea 3 Real Betis 1

CHELSEA WON 5–2 ON AGGREGATE

Great clubs have a tradition of great European nights in advanced stages of competition. Chelsea were beginning to amass these – AC Milan, February 1966; Munich 1860, March 1966; Barcelona, April 1966; Bruges, March 1971; Bruges again, March 1995. And now Real Betis, March 1998.

Yes, the League form had become at best patchy and the dream of a Premiership challenge had died, but you have to understand where Chelsea were coming from, and what was happening behind the scenes.

In 1982 the club narrowly avoided bankruptcy when Ken Bates became chairman. In 1983 relegation to the old Division Three was fended off. All through the 1980s, the battle to stay at Stamford Bridge used up copious funds and prevented the club from investing

Three days before Chelsea played Real Betis, on Monday 16 March, the Chelsea Village Hotel at the back of the Shed Umbro Stand quietly opened its doors to the public. Underneath, two restaurants and one bar were open. In the hotel, another restaurant and another bar were open. The security of Chelsea's financial future was being invested here. Chelsea Village Hotel is a 168 room four-star hotel. It is big business for a big club. Ken Bates' dream of a football club independent from the idiosyncrasies of property tycoons and insured against failure on the pitch causing financial crisis was being realized.

Real Betis, needless to say, weren't concerned with any of this. They just wanted to score a quick away goal and get back in a European tie.

Di Matteo cuts inside Merino to score Chelsea's second

in players as it would have liked. In 1991 the first million-pound players were bought. In 1992 the Royal Bank of Scotland bought the freehold of Stamford Bridge and agreed a deal with Chelsea for its purchase by the club. In 1993 Glenn Hoddle become manager and everything changed. In 1994, the first Cup Final in twenty-two years was reached and the first two-million pound player bought. In 1995 Ruud Gullit signed and everything changed once more. In 1996 Chelsea Village plc floated on the Alternative Investments Market and everything changed again as the first four-million pound player was bought. In 1997 the first silverware for twenty-six years was won and the first five-million pound player bought.

Vialli again surprised them with his tactics. He went for a solid 4–4–2 formation. Thou shalt not pass. Unfortunately, life isn't that easy.

Betis were far better going forward than defending, which made for a great night. In the first minute that wicked left foot of Jarni delivered a thirty-yard free-kick into the top corner which de Goey brilliantly tipped over.

Chelsea quickly settled and played some fine football in search of the breakthrough which would effectively kill the tie. Vialli's swerving left footer from Zola's excellent crossfield pass was well covered by Prats. Duberry couldn't quite place his free header from

Chelsea

de Goey

Sinclair   Duberry   Leboeuf   Clarke

Petrescu   Newton   Wise   Di Matteo
(Lambourde 87)

Zola   Vialli

Referee: **Bernd Heynemann** *(Germany)*

Real Betis

Alfonso

Jarni   George

Luis Fernandez   Cañas   Alexi   Marquez
(Cuellar 72)   (Oli 62)

Josete   Olias   Merino

Prats

Wise's free-kick. Zola curled an amazing free-kick from wide on the left round Prats against the far post.

The teams slowed into respect for each other, feeling each other out. Deep-lying midfielder and captain Alexis started fetching the ball from his defence and pulling all the strings. Chelsea struggled. In the twenty-first minute Betis' two danger men turned the tie upside down. Jarni's through ball was expertly flicked on by Alfonso, and Finidi George turned up in the inside-left position, and picked his spot across de Goey. Stamford Bridge went quiet.

Chelsea responded magnificently. Vialli lobbed a header from another Zola cross against the bar three minutes later. Stamford Bridge exploded back into impassioned support. Zola won the ball in Betis' half and served Di Matteo whose shot was blocked by the falling Prats. Zola was looking close to world class again.

Meanwhile, Vialli was boxing as clever as ever. He won a free-kick wide on the right for which Betis' young defender Josete was booked. Zola crossed and Sinclair escaped the same defender to head in at the near post. Sinclair had been coming in for stick from the crowd over Christmas but now he showed his mettle again.

Apart from a Jarni free-kick well defended by a seven man wall, Chelsea looked strong going into the interval. Four minutes after the break Di Matteo scored and the tie was all but over. Di Matteo always seemed the man for the big occasion. He did it all himself, dispossessing Marquez on the left, racing forward and cutting inside Merino, and then placing his shot across Prats.

Di Matteo was playing on the left, in a position even wider than the one he had looked uncomfortable in during the Charity Shield. But that allowed Wise to play through the middle. How Dennis Wise had changed! This was Chelsea's first million-pound player signed in 1991 to work the wing and present Kerry Dixon with crosses. Now he was the heart of midfield. Italy's central midfielder was playing wide for Chelsea while Chelsea's central midfielder couldn't even get into Hoddle's England squad.

And his presence ensured the tie was won. At half-time he was pushed forward onto Alexis, returning Chelsea to a midfield diamond and cutting off the Spanish team's supply. Chelsea dominated.

Meanwhile, Hoddle's central midfielders, Gascoigne of Rangers, Ince, Redknapp and McManaman of Liverpool, Batty and Lee of Newcastle and Butt of Manchester United, were all out of Europe. Villa on Tuesday and United on Wednesday had joined the earlier British exits, and only one British team was left in Europe.

Midway through the half Zola and Vialli combined once more to tear Betis apart, but Vialli slotted his shot wide. Right on time substitute Lambourde played an impressive one-two with Zola and crossed for Vialli to lay the ball back to Zola who fired a glorious left footer into the bottom corner. What a performance!

But Zola wasn't resting on his laurels as he searched for consistency. 'I said I need to play at least four or five games like that before everything is okay. This is only the second.'

Chelsea had reached their fourth European semi-final and their next game was their eighth major Cup Final. To think the club had nearly gone bankrupt sixteen years before.

	Chelsea	Real Betis
Shots on target	4	2
Woodwork	2	0
Corners	7	2
Fouls	20	11
Offsides	7	4
Bookings	1	2

Petrescu, dissent (81); Josete on Vialli (29), Marquez on Lambourde (87).

> **We started really well, we got at them immediately, then after ten minutes they got their foot on the ball. We had stages chasing the game then. All credit to them, they're a good side. But we worked hard, got behind the ball, counter-attacked well, and that was our plan. We're a top-quality team and we expect to play well against teams like this.**
>
> **Frank Sinclair**

	Chelsea	Real Betis
Goals	3	1

Sinclair (29), Di Matteo (49), Zola (90); George (20)

Assists

Zola, Vialli, Lambourde

Sunday 29 March
Wembley Stadium
77,698

Chelsea 2 Middlesbrough 0
SILVERWARE AND EUROPEAN QUALIFICATION AFTER EXTRA TIME

Glory! Chelsea's sixth major honour (one Championship, one European Cup Winners' Cup, two FA Cups and one Charity Shield) ensured UEFA Cup qualification for next season. Let's not kid ourselves. This was a pressure game because victory meant that the season was a success.

Chelsea and Middlesbrough approached the game differently. For Middlesbrough, chasing promotion back to the Premiership, it was a one-off game with a view to glory. But Chelsea were treating it professionally as a means to an end. Glory, yes, but more importantly European qualification next season. It was more than a one-off: not just win or lose, do well or bad luck. It was a passport which must be collected.

No-one played badly. Everyone was superbly professional. A job was done. Then the fun started.

Middlesbrough sprang the first surprise in the week before the Final. They bought Paul Gascoigne. He had only played one full game in an injury-plagued three months for Rangers, and his England World Cup place was under threat.

Chelsea had had ten days without a match since the Betis game with just Sinclair, Leboeuf and Flo away on international duty. Le Saux had recovered from his injury and Poyet had returned to full training following his cruciate ligament operation.

Vialli sprang the surprise of the day by leaving himself out of the Chelsea fourteen. It meant he wouldn't get a medal. But it also cleared the way for his European involvement in the remainder of the season. Everything was falling into place.

Before the start, rain fell. But Coca-Cola laid on a refreshing party atmosphere with huge puppet heads of Vialli and Wise and two Middlesbrough players, massive balloons representing each side, fireworks and songs. 'Blue Day' ruled.

There was to be no forty-three-second goal as in the FA Cup Final. In fact, after Wise had exchanged pennants with Pearson for the second time in Wembley's centre circle inside eleven months, Middlesbrough settled quickly. Merson on the right of midfield was especially direct and dangerous, taking advantage of Le Saux's rustiness to charge repetitively at Chelsea's penalty area. But there was no deadly pass.

Newton hooked away one early dangerous cross from a free-kick, but de Goey, quick to the edge of his penalty area for through balls, wasn't tested once. Sinclair was on top form, attacking all high balls into the penalty area. Middlesbrough, with their new strikers, Branca from Italy and Ricard from Columbia, simply never looked like scoring.

At the other end Chelsea slowly built up superiority. Petrescu's

Sinclair scores the first

Di Matteo puts the result beyond doubt with the second goal

thirty-yarder was just over with Schwarzer stretching, an unmarked Duberry volleyed Zola's corner over, and Di Matteo forced the first save with an angled fifteen-yarder from Hughes' pass.

From the twentieth minute Chelsea stepped up a gear. Le Saux got back at Merson, burst outside him and crossed just behind Hughes. Hughes turned and brilliantly half-volleyed a thunderous effort that seemed a certain goal. Schwarzer was magnificent in palming the shot away, and Hughes held his head in anguish.

A minute later Di Matteo attacked down the right, leaving Vickers struggling, and his cross was deflected by Pearson to Zola whose left-foot shot was narrowly wide.

Another minute later and Zola on the left turned his compatriot Festa inside out with a wiggle and a hop before picking out Hughes with his cross. His strong downward header was brilliantly blocked by Schwarzer. Again, Hughes buried his head in his huge forearms. Schwarzer was keeping Middlesbrough in it. From the resulting corner Di Matteo's twenty-yarder was just wide.

Middlesbrough pulled themselves together and held out comfortably until half-time. In the first fifteen minutes of the second-half they had a couple of chances. Sinclair saved the situation on both occasions. First he cut across after Merson had raced inside Le Saux and swept the ball away from him, and a minute later he did even better, running even faster to get across his area and stop Branca taking advantage of former Blues

> *Funny, we seem to do things in twos, me and Eddie. We've been together at the club a long time and the first thing he said to me was: "I can't believe you've had to go and copy me, scoring a goal the year after!" He's as happy for me as I am, and last year it was vice-versa.*
>
> **Frank Sinclair**

captain Townsend's pass. Sinclair was proving to be Chelsea's outstanding player.

Just before the hour Zola nearly won the afternoon. He played the ball in from the left to Petrescu on the edge of the area, received a perfect lay-off and thundered a curling, dipping twenty-five-yarder over Schwarzer and against the crossbar. Now it was his turn to hold his head.

Middlesbrough introduced Gascoigne for Ricard. The extra midfielder gave them more of the ball, but manager Bryan Robson had asked him to play just ahead of midfield and instead he played deep. Merson saw less of the ball, and Middlesbrough still didn't penetrate.

Gascoigne was quickly booked for taking Zola's legs. Wise was quickly booked for jumping in two-footed at Gascoigne. 'I just wanted him to know I was there,' Dennis twinkled. The arrival of the England superstar had encouraged Wise to step his game up a gear. Still nowhere near full fitness, he began to take charge of midfield.

Chelsea's only scare came three minutes from the end. They had been in charge without truly dominating, and Middlesbrough's only chance was to nick the game late. Maddison's header across goal just eluded the leaping Branca as Gascoigne's free-kick stopped some hearts for the only time during the afternoon.

By now Chelsea had made two changes. Clarke had come on for

Chelsea's manager and captain share the moment of triumph

Petrescu and gone to the left of defence, allowing Le Saux in particular but also Sinclair to push forward and challenge Middlesbrough's numerical supremacy in midfield. And Flo had come on for Hughes to run at Middlesbrough.

Four minutes into extra time Chelsea scored. There was something inevitable about it. What was surprising was the name of the scorer. Sinclair took advantage of Gascoigne and Merson mucking up an ambitious one-two in their own half, fed Zola and kept running. Zola sent Wise away wide, and although his first touch wasn't good he reached the ball before it crossed the goal

The glory boys

line and hooked in a telling cross which the charging Sinclair leapt to head down with great force. Schwarzer got a hand to it but it brushed past him.

Sinclair dived on the ground screaming: 'I don't believe it, I don't believe it, I don't believe it,' and his colleagues dived on top of him. Zola cried out: 'You have to believe it!' and Sinclair screamed back: 'I don't believe it!' But it was true.

Branca managed one shot from Merson's pass that de Goey had to dive to hold, but this was Chelsea's trophy now. Wise, in total charge, raced half the length of the field before being tripped by Gascoigne just outside the area. Gascoigne was lucky not to be sent off. From the free-kick Leboeuf's thunderbolt went just wide.

The second goal, a minute into the second period of extra time, followed an outstanding move. Leboeuf's forty-yard pass was brilliantly headed square by Zola to Wise, who quickly sent Flo away. The big man raced into the box and his shot was turned aside by Schwarzer. Zola miscued the corner, but it fooled Mustoe

who slipped and Di Matteo tip-toed in to sidefoot home. Di Matteo had served up the goods again. He ran to Zola and the two Italians knelt and embraced.

Di Matteo should have had another when Flo again attacked down the left to leave Pearson confused and laid the ball back, but the charging Italian turned it over.

Chelsea played out the last ten minutes as they had played out the end of the FA Cup Final – pass, pass, pass, stroll and accelerate, pass.

In an emotional post-match ceremony, Wise invited Vialli to collect the Cup, and in his suit the manager did just that. The lap of honour was again climaxed with the group charge from the halfway line followed by a group dive. No Cups for twenty-six years and now two in eleven months. Zola's continuous punching of the air summed it all up.

Chelsea had rarely had it this good. And there was more to come. Blue Day? No, Blue Year.

> '*We were surprised he didn't pick himself, the number of goals he's got this season, but it's his choice, he's the manager. We just felt he should go up himself because we all felt he should be part of it.*'
>
> **Dennis Wise**

> '*We were a bit unlucky in the first ninety minutes but we were more ruthless in extra-time. Ruudi took the team to the semi-final, so if we have won today it's also because of Ruudi, so I think he'll be happy. I am very pleased that Chelsea is getting used to winning things. To win something mustn't be an exception, it must be a routine.*'
>
> **Gianluca Vialli**

Celebrations continue in the Wembley dressing room bath

	Chelsea	Middlesbrough
Shots on target	6	2
Woodwork	1	0
Corners	8	4
Fouls	21	20
Offsides	2	5
Bookings	4	2

M Hughes, foul (34), Le Saux, dissent (40), Wise, foul (75), Leboeuf, foul (87); Townsend on Wise (52); Gascoigne on Zola (70).

	Chelsea	Middlesbrough
Goals	2	0

Sinclair (94), Di Matteo (106)

Assists

Wise, Zola

Thursday 2 April
Romeo Menti Stadium
19,319

Vicenza 1 Chelsea 0

IT ISN'T EASY WINNING DOUBLES

No rest for Cup Final winners. No parade, and little celebration. There was a Cup Final banquet after the Coca-Cola victory on Sunday evening, the first to be held at The Galleria in Chelsea Village, but then there was training on Monday and Tuesday, and on Wednesday the squad flew to Verona and travelled by coach to Vicenza.

Vicenza's was a small ground with a capacity just over 21,000. They were struggling against relegation from Serie A. They had been in Europe only once before after finishing runners-up in the days of Paolo Rossi, and they went out in the first round of the UEFA Cup to Dukla Prague.

So it was no exaggeration when Vicenza coach Guidolin Francesco called this: 'The match of history.'

were still struggling for absolute match fitness, and now Sinclair had suffered a groin strain at Wembley that was to trouble him for some time.

Vicenza had quality in their ranks. Striker Luiso wasn't far off the Italy squad and had overtaken Vialli as the competition's top scorer. His young partner Zauli, wandering free between midfield and attack, had helped turn their season round from what once seemed certain relegation. In midfield Ambrosini was a good passer and Ambrosetti a fast and direct winger.

But there was nothing for a fit and tuned in Chelsea to fear. Tonight, we did not see that Chelsea.

Perhaps Chelsea gave the Italians too much respect. Wise thought so, although Vialli didn't. He believed the tactics were right. His

Vialli's header was cleared off the line

Chelsea were tired. One hundred and twenty minutes of Wembley is energy sapping, and never mind that this was a European semi-final – it was the forty-fifth game of the season.

Problems lingered: Wise couldn't train, Duberry and Newton

strategy was the same as in Spain, but his personnel had one crucial change. He himself replaced Flo as the sole attacker. The problem was that he lacked Flo's pace and size. Flo hadn't just scored two wonderful goals in Seville, he had led the line like a wily target man.

Brivio

Mendez   Belotti   Dicara   Viviani

Schenardi   Di Carlo   Ambrosini   Ambrosetti
(Stovini 74)   (Beghetto 74)

Zauli   Luiso
(Firmani 87)

Referee: **Manuel Diaz Vega** (Spain)

Vialli

Zola   Petrescu
(Morris 89)   (Flo 59)

Di Matteo   Wise   Newton

Le Saux   Leboeuf   Duberry   Clarke

de Goey

There was one other difference in Italy. Vicenza were far better defensively than Betis even though they were not nearly as good offensively.

So Chelsea played the wary European travellers and didn't give things a go. They were quickly on the back foot. Zauli's powerful free header from Ambrosetti's inswinging corner almost caught de Goey going the wrong way, but the big Dutchman flung himself to the near post and brilliantly palmed the ball away at full stretch when it seemed to be behind him. It was one of the season's great saves.

But three minutes later it seemed irrelevant. Left-back Viviani's long ball found Zauli stealing in behind Newton and as Duberry closed in he checked back behind Newton, evaded Duberry and shot with something of a miscue across de Goey before Leboeuf could arrive. In 1971 Chelsea won the first leg of a victorious Cup Winners' Cup semi-final 1–0 with a Derek Smethurst mis-hit. Surely a historic irony was not to be paid back.

Chelsea didn't respond to falling behind. Zola playing wide was tired and out of place, Petrescu was ineffectual and Vialli was inconsequential. Defensively the Blues remained stretched. Leboeuf and Duberry blocked crucially after Ambrosetti's free-kick had rebounded off the wall, then Vialli blocked Viviani's effort after de Goey had punched out Schenardi's wide free-kick. Ten minutes before half-time Duberry's awful pass from defence gave Zauli the ball and Chelsea were so lucky when his pass to Luiso found the striker offside.

The Vicenza supporters were brilliant, all waving flags and singing non-stop. Before the second-half their rendition of 'When a Child is Born' – goodness knows what words they used – was awesome.

Vicenza remained on top for an hour. Di Matteo was harshly booked for tripping Zauli which meant suspension from the second leg. He was Chelsea's first suspension for two bookings in Europe this season. And given that he was the proven big-match man, that could prove costly.

But de Goey was also proving himself the big-match man. When Luiso superbly laid off a long ball to Zauli and raced onto an equally brilliant first-time return, his startling top-corner twenty-yarder looked a certain goal. De Goey soared and stretched and tipped it round. He was turning into a Cup hero. Arsenal away, Betis away, and now Vicenza.

That incident signalled the end of Vicenza's domination. Chelsea brought on Flo for Petrescu and he was immediately more direct. Minutes later a weary Zola raced in from the right and tried to cross for Vialli, but his slice caught Brivio out and bounced off the nearside of the post.

Two more minutes later and Vialli soared to Zola's corner only to see his excellent downward header cleared off the line by Ambrosetti. A little later Wise ran free from Zola's delicate free-kick but chose to cross rather than shoot from an acute angle. The chance went to waste.

Vicenza had one more chance when Newton blocked Di Carlo's shot after a free-kick, but in the end the Blues could be thankful not to have fallen further behind in the first hour, and disappointed not to have equalized in the last half-hour. As in the Coca-Cola semi-final first leg, they had played poorly but got a result that still gave them a chance.

	Vicenza	Chelsea
Shots on target	6	4
Woodwork	0	1
Corners	3	5
Fouls	15	21
Offsides	6	1
Bookings	3	2

Dicara on Vialli (53), Zauli, play-acting (72), Di Carlo on Duberry (81); Leboeuf, dissent (47), Di Matteo, foul (49).

> *The important thing is qualification is still open. We played exactly the same as in Betis but we couldn't do the job we did there. We played long balls, that was our purpose, but unfortunately it didn't work so well. Sometimes this happens. But we can still do it.*
>
> Gianfranco Zola

	Vicenza	Chelsea
Goals	1	0

Zauli (15)

Derby County 0 Chelsea 1

FIRST AWAY WIN AFTER EUROPEAN TIE

Priorities were clear. With a UEFA Cup place guaranteed, winning the European Cup Winners' Cup was the most important target of the season. All the right words about the need for doing well in the League were secondary to winning two more Cup Winners' Cup games. A double Cup year would be the most glorious thing Chelsea had ever done.

De Goey, Duberry, Le Saux, the suspended Wise and Zola weren't merely rested. They didn't even travel.

Clarke, playing his 413th Chelsea game, was captain. He was now Chelsea's fifth highest all-time appearance maker. At the start of the season his form was as good as ever, but the calf strains had taken their toll, and he looked to find it harder and harder to return in the middle of a season from injury. But the thirty-four-year-old could be relied upon to do a job wherever asked, to put the team's needs first at any time. The old electric pace had gone, but the knowledge was so immense that he could cope with any situation.

Today, for the first time in his Chelsea career, he was asked to man-mark someone. Ironically, the last time he had done a man-marking job had been for St Mirren against Gordon Durie, later to become his close friend at Chelsea. Today it was Derby's Italian playmaker, Baiano.

Baiano had been having a wonderful season. But Derby were out of sorts. The first two times he got the ball Baiano nutmegged Clarke. On one of those occasions his left-sided cross had Granville and Wanchope challenging in the area, but fortunately for Chelsea both just missed the ball.

But that was that for Baiano. Clarke just cancelled him out with a marvellous performance. Derby had nowhere to go. Their manager Jim Smith admitted it. 'We didn't know how to break them down. We were taking twenty or thirty passes to get into their box. If anything we had too much possession.'

As Clarke was successfully chasing late rainbows, Jon Harley was leaving home for the first time. The eighteen-year-old made his debut at left wing-back, the position he had filled for the reserves and youth team all season.

It had been an outstanding year for the former FA School of Excellence youngster. He immediately showed off his silky skills and never once looked out of place. As Clarke dented Derby's offensive hopes, Harley killed them off altogether. His thirty-seventh-minute cross provided Mark Hughes with the chance to lob a header over Hoult for his tenth goal of the season. Now Vialli, Flo, Zola and Hughes were all in double figures.

It was an excellent move started by Clarke's chip forward from the right-back position, expertly controlled and thwacked out to the left by Hughes. Harley's first touch was perfect, and he ran forward before crossing early.

Debut Jon Harley

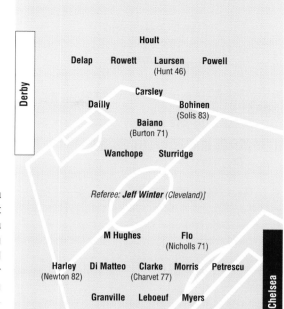

Derby

Hoult

Delap   Rowett   Laursen   Powell
(Hunt 46)

Carsley

Dailly   Bohinen
(Solis 83)

Baiano
(Burton 71)

Wanchope   Sturridge

*Referee: **Jeff Winter** (Cleveland)]*

Chelsea

M Hughes   Flo
(Nicholls 71)

Harley   Di Matteo   Clarke   Morris   Petrescu
(Newton 82)   (Charvet 77)

Granville   Leboeuf   Myers

Kharine

A lead was no less than Chelsea deserved. Derby were pretty but not penetrating and that allowed Chelsea to play more of a shorter passing game than of late. The experienced spine of sweeper Leboeuf, anchor midfielder Clarke, attacking midfielder Di Matteo and centre-forward Hughes was outstanding.

The less experienced players around them benefited. On the right of defence the left-footed Myers barely put a foot wrong. On the left of the back three, back in his old Cambridge United position, Granville was faultless. Morris looked more like the youngster with the world at his feet again.

After eleven minutes Di Matteo nicked the ball off Carsley in the centre circle, spotted Hoult off his line and delivered a sixty-yarder that was only just wide. After half an hour he nicked the ball again and sent Hughes away up the left. Hughes cut inside Rowett and his shot bounced off the bar.

In the second-half Di Matteo nicked the ball off Baiano and Flo careered away, but his feeding of Hughes was a bit too tight to defeat Hoult. Flo was having one of those running into cul-de-sac days.

On the hour Derby woke up and Delap's well-struck lob was brilliantly tipped over by Kharine — more evidence of his improving fitness.

With twenty minutes to go Jim Smith gave up on Baiano and substituted him. The Italian turned to his conqueror Clarke and shook hands with him. It was a lovely moment. Derby switched to 4–3–3 so Chelsea switched to 4–4–2 and held out comfortably. They showed excellent composure. Di Matteo picked up a cracked rib late in the game, but the important thing was that Chelsea were camped in fourth place and a whole lot of squad players had picked up a win bonus.

	Derby	Chelsea
Shots on target	2	2
Woodwork	0	1
Corners	6	2
Fouls	14	13
Offsides	5	10
Bookings	0	1

Granville, foul (13).

> **The players showed me this afternoon they're good enough to play for Chelsea. I can rely on them even if some of the key players aren't available. There's plenty of nice lads with fresh legs ready to do the job. Jon Harley was magnificent in his first match. He played like a very experienced player.**
>
> **Gianluca Vialli**

Hughes leaps to head the winner

	Derby	Chelsea
Goals	0	1
M Hughes (36)		
Assist		
Harley		

Wednesday 8 April
Elland Road
37,276

Leeds United 3 Chelsea 1

SIXTH DEFEAT IN SEVEN PREMIERSHIP AWAY GAMES

Pride is undoubtedly different to a supporter than to a club employee. Everyone in the club talked about finishing higher in the Premiership than the previous season, sixth, but finishing as European winners was far more important now.

Tell that to a supporter on a wet night in Yorkshire after a lousy trip up the motorway. Most Chelsea supporters, caught in tortoise-like traffic, arrived in a rush for kick-off. I was one. For only the second time in the season I forsook the press box to join the travelling throng behind the goal. It was the end where Leeds were presented with their first two goals! There was a great deal of disenchantment in the crowd.

Chelsea would sink dangerously close to a finish of sixth, as in the previous season, if they lost. And if they lost in the European Cup Winners' Cup, you would have to say that sixth and the Coca-Cola Cup was not as good as sixth and the FA Cup. Not just pride, but progress was at stake here.

But everything was focused on winning against Vicenza next week. Petrescu was allowed to fly off to play for Romania where he was captain for the second time while Leboeuf was given a deserved rest.

At sweeper Lee started his first game in nearly eighteen months since breaking his leg. As with Kharine before him, he was very rusty.

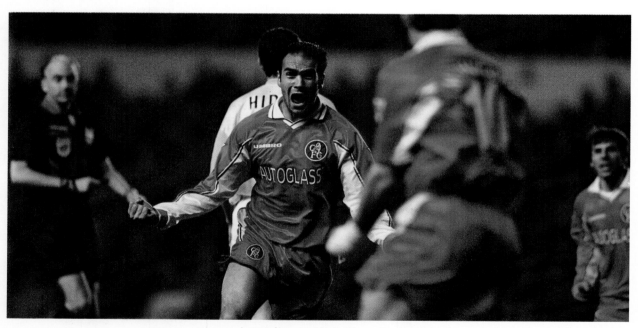

Laurent Charvet celebrates his equalizer

Why have Chelsea got such a lousy record at Leeds? No other ground gives such foundation to the accusation of southern softies as Leeds. How many times do Chelsea roll over and die at Elland Road?

Okay, so the Premiership was losing importance to the club. But there was still a great deal of pride to play for. In Chelsea's ninety-three-year history they had finished in the top four only four times – top once, in 1955, and third three times, in 1920, 1965 and 1970. Even fifth place had been achieved only once since 1970. If this team was to be looked upon as the greatest Chelsea side, then a high League place still needed claiming.

Leeds would leapfrog Chelsea into fourth place if they won.

Both sides played 3–5–2, but where Vialli had said that Chelsea would outplay Crystal Palace man for man by adopting the same formation, tonight they lost man for man. Leeds deserved to win.

Three questions were raised. Were Chelsea too soft for the tough sides? Why was away form in the Premiership so dismal? Starting with defeat at Southampton on Boxing Day, the record after Elland Road read: played seven, won one, drawn none, lost six, scored four, conceded thirteen. And why could Chelsea not beat a team in the top five? Arsenal in the second leg of the Coca-Cola Cup under the extraordinary circumstances of Vialli's first game in charge following Gullit's ousting was the only occasion since before last season's FA

Leeds

Martyn

Hiden Wetherall Molenaar
(Haaland 46)

Kelly Halle Radebe Bowyer Harte

Hasselbaink Kewell

Referee: **David Elleray** (Harrow, Middlesex)

Zola M Hughes
(Flo 62)

Le Saux Wise Newton Morris Charvet
(Lambourde 81) (P Hughes 81)

Myers Lee Duberry

Kharine

Chelsea

Cup semi-final that they had beaten a top-five team.

It was just as well Chelsea had done so that night. Arsenal's surge up the table was taking them beyond the apparently uncatchable Manchester United to the Championship. If only Chelsea had not stumbled for so long from mid-December, this *could* have been the Blues' year. Indeed, Arsenal were surging to the League and FA Cup double. Hell, Chelsea prevented them from winning the Treble!

Now Chelsea had to land their own first double, a Cup double. But first, they had to get back some consistency. And that didn't happen at Elland Road.

Dutch tank Hasselbaink scored his first after six minutes. He turned away from Duberry's clumsy rush to take a diagonal throw-in forward, swivelled past Myers as he tried to close in, and hit a twenty-five-yarder through the dreadful conditions with a bump and a bounce in off the post. Kharine, stretching wide, would surely not have been beaten from that distance before his injury.

Chelsea equalized four minutes later. Duberry organized positions in Leeds' penalty area before delivering a long throw onto Hughes' head which was tucked back for Charvet to fire a cannon of a half-volley inside the far post. Charvet was looking a very useful penalty area player.

Leeds retook the lead eleven minutes later after Myers had unnecessarily fouled Kewell. Kelly's wide free-kick

	Leeds	Chelsea
Shots on target	5	3
Woodwork	0	1
Corners	4	3
Fouls	12	20
Offsides	1	4
Bookings	1	2

Wetherall on M Hughes (8), Radebe on Zola (47); M Hughes foul (51).

> **We wanted to match their toughness, we did that, but not for ninety-five minutes. If you look at our record we've lost too many matches against teams who are not as good as us at playing football. I wouldn't swap one of my players for any of their players. Yet we lost 3–1. We need to improve our attitude when the opposition is tough. This is the only way we can improve to win the Premiership next season.**
>
> Gianluca Vialli

found Wetherall getting away from Duberry for a free header.

One great passing move involving half the team ended with a poor Myers touch as he burst into the penalty area, but lack of organization at the back was the main problem as marking and offside play kept breaking down.

Leeds extended their lead two minutes into the second-half when a Harte cross was allowed to bounce in the six-yard box and the unmarked Hasselbaink headed past Kharine at the far post. It was a controversial goal because Chelsea had lost possession just after Zola was fouled. Referee Elleray had waved play on and then booked Radebe for the foul before kicking off.

Chelsea's one moment of hope was when Wise, combative as ever, floated a twenty-yard free-kick which Martyn brilliantly turned onto the bar. But Leeds always looked more likely to score a fourth than Chelsea a second. At least Chelsea played more football as Lee found his passing game, but Leeds were adamant they would not be passed, and they weren't.

To make it a bad night all round Bernard Lambourde was arrested in the dressing room after the game following allegations that he had indecently assaulted a woman working at the hotel where the team was staying. It cast a shadow over the remainder of his season as he was trying to force himself on to the bench for European glory. He wasn't cleared until the week before the last League game of the season. His innocent verdict never got the publicity of his original charge.

	Leeds	Chelsea
Goals	3	1

Hasselbaink (6, 47), Wetherall (21); Charvet (10)

Assists
Duberry, M Hughes

Saturday 11 April
Stamford Bridge
34,149

Chelsea 2 Tottenham Hotspur 0

NINETEEN SUCCESSIVE UNDEFEATED GAMES AGAINST TOTTENHAM

Good Friday started at the training ground with a meeting and a forty-five minute video of the first-half at Leeds. Team play was discussed. Some players preferred three at the back, some preferred 4–4–2. Everyone knew that Vialli preferred 4–3–3, and with Laudrup joining the club next season that remained a long-term likelihood.

Once again the management stressed their belief that three at the back did not win trophies in England. You needed the more solid four at the back.

Just as sixteen months before when Gullit had gone with 3–5–2 every game and Chelsea had found themselves, now Vialli went with 4–4–2 or a variation on it. Would Chelsea find themselves?

Vialli had said after defeat at Leeds that he wished to play his European selection for Vicenza against Tottenham, all except in goal. But Kharine complained of a stiff knee following the game so

de Goey was brought back anyway. Newton was rested. Zola didn't play.

Was this the European team? The players not chosen may have steeled themselves for training to prove their worth over the next few days. On the bench there was the wonderful sight of Gustavo Poyet returning just six months after his cruciate ligament injury. He had enjoyed forty-five minutes of one reserve game and seventy minutes of another, scoring with his last touch in the latter.

With Di Matteo suspended on Thursday against Vicenza, Poyet was pencilled in for half an hour here whatever the circumstances.

How do you better the 6–1 win over Tottenham in December? You don't, but with Tottenham still attached to the relegation battle, that didn't matter. Just to keep the record going against Tottenham, eighteen successive games without defeat, and to prepare properly for Europe, was enough.

Tottenham were as poor as their League position suggested.

Vialli scores his 18th of the season

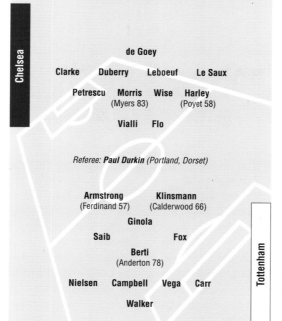

Chelsea

de Goey

Clarke   Duberry   Leboeuf   Le Saux

Petrescu   Morris   Wise   Harley
            (Myers 83)   (Poyet 58)

Vialli   Flo

*Referee: **Paul Durkin** (Portland, Dorset)*

Armstrong   Klinsmann
(Ferdinand 57)   (Calderwood 66)

Ginola

Saib   Fox

Berti
(Anderton 78)

Nielsen   Campbell   Vega   Carr

Walker

Tottenham

Surprisingly, they didn't even take up their full quota of tickets. They were in a bad way. For Chelsea, Harley was given another chance and Morris kept his place.

Once Ginola's early dash had finished with Clarke deflecting Nielsen's cross for a corner, Chelsea had what shots there were. The game was perfectly encapsulated when Clarke slipped on crossing and Campbell completely missed the ball, leaving Vialli to try a lob shot which Walker easily held.

With Duberry still not back to his pre-injury best, it was interesting to see England's Campbell so out of sorts in this desperate Tottenham side. England's best young defender? Play on, Doobs!

Morris was continuing to improve in midfield, looking sharper, which with his small stature was so crucial to his game. A one-two with Vialli saw him burst through the middle and feed Flo with Campbell again struggling. Walker scrambled Flo's effort round for a corner, and from that Flo had another shot blocked.

Harley's twenty-yarder sizzled just wide five minutes before half-time, but he didn't look as comfortable as an out-and-out midfielder as he had at wing-back.

He was substituted by Poyet, as planned, just before the hour. During his time out Poyet had appeared on the pitch several times to present various items and every time he had been greeted with huge warmth and applause by the crowd. Now he received another standing ovation. What a fillip!

A minute earlier Duberry had escaped punishment when his reckless challenge on Klinsmann was not regarded as a penalty. It happened just after a fit again Les Ferdinand had replaced an angry Chris Armstrong, and now Klinsmann, no longer looking the world class player of Euro 96, limped off. Tottenham were struggling.

Chelsea turned the screw. Poyet looked as though he had never been away. Wise, now running the show, shot just wide, Petrescu ghosted round Walker but the angle was too acute to score, Flo was stopped by Campbell's last-ditch tackle as he strode square along the goal line, Vialli was refused a penalty from Nielsen's challenge and Walker escaped a handball when he saved on the edge of his area.

The first goal came on seventy-three minutes. Morris did well when Tottenham cleared a cross, not delivering the obvious ball back wide but threading one to Vialli in the area. Vialli's delicious backflick gave Flo a simple sidefoot in.

The second came with four minutes to go. Leboeuf headed away from Ferdinand, Flo raced off down the right, fed Petrescu square on the edge of the penalty area, and his pass left Vialli with a sidefoot in for his eighteenth goal of the season.

Poyet was delighted. 'I feel good. I enjoy,' he shouted in his improving English. 'When I come on the pitch we're staying 0–0, after, we win.'

In the last minute Vega lobbed a header against the top of the bar, but Chelsea had enjoyed a stroll and a clean sheet before the big game. As Leeds had lost at relegation-threatened Everton, Chelsea had returned to fourth place while Tottenham sunk deeper in the mire. That made life better for the Chelsea supporters who had travelled to Leeds. A hell of a lot better.

> **We felt that it was a very important match for us as well. We can't go on losing in the League games. We needed that win for our confidence. It was important.**
>
> **Tore Andre Flo**

	Chelsea	Tottenham
Shots on target	6	1
Woodwork	0	1
Corners	9	9
Fouls	15	11
Offsides	5	4
Bookings	0	1
Berti on Wise (23).		

	Chelsea	Tottenham
Goals	2	0
Flo (73), Vialli (86)		
Assists		
Morris, Vialli, Flo, Petrescu		

Thursday 16 April
Stamford Bridge
33,810

Chelsea 3 Vicenza 1

CHELSEA WON 3–2 ON AGGREGATE

There have been many great nights at Stamford Bridge, several great seasons and a fair number of top European nights. Tonight this Chelsea side established itself as one of the greats. This was as good as it gets. Were you there? If you weren't, you can't imagine what you missed. If you were, wasn't it everything you dream of?

Let's not pretend it was the greatest football of all time. It wasn't. But Chelsea scored three great goals when time was short and the result was everything.

For the second time in the competition Chelsea went two goals down. At Tromsø, however, it was two goals down in the first leg, and two goals down against a poor side not practiced in the art of defending.

Vicenza were a disciplined Italian outfit. They knew how to nick an away goal and hang on. And an away goal was all they needed. Vialli stressed to his side that 1–0 at ninety minutes would do. That would still give Chelsea half an hour at home to work the winner.

He should have known better. This was Chelsea. Nothing has ever been easy for Chelsea.

The week started badly. Petrescu went down with a nasty virus and was ruled out. So Morris, still only nineteen, was given his first European start. The good news was that Poyet was ready to start.

Unlike Tottenham the previous Saturday, Vicenza fans took over the whole of the East Stand lower tier. They sang and chanted and backed their team magnificently. What a noise they made. And it was all in tune! Why can't English fans sing in tune?

Chelsea came out with passion and toughness but it was Vicenza who started cleverly. If Chelsea were to win through they would need some heroes. De Goey emerged as one after six minutes. Ambrosetti's cross from the left found Schenardi unmarked in the area, but de Goey spread himself and smothered the ball. Chelsea fans went quiet. The tension was awful.

Zola had got the forward vote, along with Vialli, and he was superb. Out of the Italy squad for their last two games, if he wanted to go to the World Cup he had to impress. His pass fed Wise on the left, the captain ducked back inside a defender and crossed for Vialli to head powerfully goalwards. A roar erupted, but the goalkeeper, Brivio, punched away brilliantly. Then the keeper turned Zola's fierce near-post shot round after Clarke and Morris had set him up.

Chelsea were knocking the ball forward early and long, but it wasn't a tactic especially suited for the two small forwards. In the first thirty-one minutes the combative home team committed ten fouls. The Italian choir roared. Chelsea fans were quiet.

Just before the half hour mark the speedy Ambrosetti fired a thirty-yarder that de Goey couldn't hold but Leboeuf cleared. Just after the half hour disaster struck. Zauli took advantage of Duberry's poor clearance to dribble round Newton and lob the defence. Once again the offside organization was a mess. Lebeouf raced forward and into le Saux, Clarke played everyone onside, so Schenardi and Luiso were left all alone, and Luiso buried his fifteen-yarder in the top corner.

Two down and, with an away goal conceded, Chelsea now needed three in the hour remaining. With an away goal scored there could now be no extra-time. The next fifty-nine minutes would decide how good Chelsea's season would be. 'It's one of them, isn't it,' said Dennis Wise afterwards. 'You think…"Oh no!," but you know if you score quickly you can win.'

Chelsea scored quickly, and what a finish it was. Brivio punched out a brave Le Saux cross to the edge of the area where Zola controlled the clearance and fired a superb low left-footer back. Brivio dived to bash that away, but Poyet, arriving like a steam train, threw himself sideways and somehow kept the ball down and directed it into the goal. His first start, his first strike. But he didn't go Poyet crazy. He simply retrieved the ball from the net and returned to the halfway line.

Two minutes later a crucial incident happened. Ambrosini fouled Zola and was booked. It was his second booking and he would now miss the Final if Vicenza won. His focus died.

But Chelsea still had to survive the remainder of the first-half. Duberry blocked Di Carlo's shot and Luiso's header with the

Zola scores his first headed goal for Chelsea

Chelsea

de Goey

Clarke   Duberry   Leboeuf   Le Saux

Morris   Newton   Wise   Poyet
(Charvet 70) (M Hughes 70)

Zola   Vialli
(Myers 80)

*Referee: **Marc Batta** (France)*

Luiso

Zauli

Ambrosetti   Ambrosini   Di Carlo   Schenardi
(Otero 80) (Di Napoli 80)

Viviani   Dicara   Belotti   Mendez
(Stovini 61)

Brivio

Vicenza

defence at sixes and sevens, and right on half-time Leboeuf raced back to clear off the line after Luiso had poked the ball past de Goey. No wonder the crowd was quiet.

The second goal, five minutes into the second-half was unbelievable. Vialli was arguing with the linesman on the right touchline when Ambrosini gave the ball away to him. Vialli sped down the flank like a teenage right-winger and delivered a head-high bullet cross which was met by the sprinting, leaping Zola whose header flew over Brivio and into the net. It was his first headed goal for Chelsea and it was magnificent.

But Vicenza still led on the away goals rule. The home crowd now swung into top volume as Chelsea surged forward and Vialli was just wide from Wise's cross. Another great Vialli wide run led to Le Saux's stubbed shot which fell for Wise. He turned and fired straight at Brivio. He should have scored. He held his head in his hands.

Vicenza went close from a free-kick – another away goal would seal the tie for them – but really it was all Chelsea. Long balls forward. Get at 'em and up 'em. You'd never guess this was an Italian manager!

With twenty minutes left Rix made a double substitution and switched to 3–4–3. A goal was needed. Enter the expert of rescuing lost causes, Mark Hughes. The first three times the ball came to him he hurled himself at defenders and conceded fouls. Muscle and fire. He was lucky not to get booked.

Then de Goey launched another long ball downfield and Hughes jumped to

head it over Belotti and as he landed he had turned and was chasing. Belotti was still looking for it when Hughes, fifteen yards out in the inside-left position, launched a volley. The ball rocketed into the far corner. Stamford Bridge exploded. West London, all of London, Europe and the world must have heard. Chelsea were in the lead with fifteen minutes to go.

When de Goey had to save from Ambrosetti following a corner, Rix sent on Myers for Zola, intent on shutting things up with a return to 4–4–2. Zola sat on the bench and cried: 'Ye-e-e-esss!' for all of England and Italy to see. Roll on the Final.

Two minutes from time Ambrosini fouled Vialli and was sent off. In stoppage time de Goey literally saved the season. Substitute Di Napoli ran at Clarke and Duberry, crossed wickedly, and with Luiso closing in the big goalkeeper brilliantly dived out to fingertip the ball away. 'What a save!' cried Dennis Wise.

The whistle went and the players jumped on the triumphant goalkeeper. But they had all been heroes. Chelsea were into their second European final, and they stayed on the pitch a long, long time celebrating with an ecstatic crowd.

'We touched the Final with one hand,' said a sad Vicenza coach. 'We played on a very difficult pitch against a team who deserves to be in the Final. We all know, perhaps better than you, Vialli is a great player. He is lucky but he's a winner.'

	Chelsea	Vicenza
Shots on target	10	6
Corners	9	4
Fouls	27	18
Offsides	3	3
Bookings	0	1
Luiso, not withdrawing ten yards (25).		
Sending off	0	1
Ambrosini, two bookings (36) and (88).		

One of the tops. Up there with the FA Cup and Coca-Cola Cup Finals. We've shown everyone what we can do, we've taken the step forward in Europe. I think the fans have to be over the moon about what we've done this year. But it ain't over yet. We've got the Final to look forward to and we know we can win it.

Dennis Wise

	Chelsea	Vicenza
Goals	3	1
Poyet (34), Zola (50), M Hughes (75); Luiso (31)		
Assists		
Zola, Vialli		

Sunday 19 April
Stamford Bridge
29,075

Chelsea 1 Sheffield Wednesday 0

THREE WINS IN A ROW FOR THE FIRST TIME UNDER VIALLI

Two minutes from time against Vicenza, Dennis Wise felt a tear in his thigh. He limped off and received treatment from Mike Banks. Chelsea had already made the three substitutions allowed and needed eleven men on the pitch to defend their lead. So Wise went back on and toughed out the remaining time.

It takes a couple of days for such an injury to calm down and the damage be assessed, but it was immediately clear that he was unlikely to make the European Cup Winners' Cup Final. Several alternative treatments were discussed, but by the time Sunday came round the decision had been made that he would go to Italy later in the week for treatment.

It is impossible to overestimate Wise's importance to the team. No-one had seen how badly he was injured so Chelsea said publicly that he had a dead leg and was resting his still injured toe. He couldn't climb stairs or walk without a dreadful limp. But he was allowed to concentrate on recovering in peace.

The following week Gianfranco Zola was to tear a groin muscle and media attention focused on his progress to the Final. But right up until the last few days Wise was as big a doubt.

Chelsea went into the weekend game with a big milestone within their grasp. The three goals against Vicenza had taken them to ninety-nine for the season. One hundred goals had only been achieved four times before.

Frank Leboeuf blasts the penalty winner and Chelsea's one hundredth goal of the season

Chelsea

Kharine

Clarke   Duberry   Leboeuf   Granville
(P Hughes 80)

Charvet   Di Matteo   Newton   Harley
(Morris 62)

Flo   M Hughes
(Nicholls 69)

Referee: Gary Willard (Worthing, Sussex)

Booth Di Canio

Rudi   Stefanovic   Atherton   Carbone
(Pembridge 13)

Hinchcliffe   Walker   Thome   Barrett
(Magilton 84)

Pressman

Sheffield Wednesday

The milestone took twenty-two minutes to reach. Clarke's long ball was flicked on by Mark Hughes and as Barrett moved to defend Flo nipped ahead of him. Barrett wrapped himself round the striker to make contact with the ball, Flo went down and referee Willard pointed to the penalty spot. Wednesday boss Ron Atkinson was furious. 'If that was a penalty I'll plait sawdust.'

Get plaiting, Ron. Leboeuf blasted Chelsea's 100th goal of the season high to Pressman's right and maintained his 100 percent Chelsea record from the spot.

Either side of the goal Wednesday were unlucky. Rudi drove a rising shot against Kharine's post after the goalkeeper had punched out Booth's unchallenged cross, and Carbone's brilliant overhead kick after Booth had nodded on Pressman's downfield punt rattled against the bar.

But the truth was Wednesday weren't very good, and with both goalkeepers hoisting long balls down the pitch neither was the game.

Astonishingly, the second–half started with both teams deciding to play football. The strong wind had dropped and play improved. Chelsea had the better of the half without producing anything to get too excited about. Di Matteo crossed against the outside of the near post and had another shot deflected just wide, Charvet went close and Flo forced Pressman to block. At the other end Kharine turned round Di Canio's fine strike.

Considering that Poyet, Le Saux, Zola and Vialli were all absent, a second successive win after Europe, another clean sheet and a third win on the trot – the first time this had happened under Vialli – represented a good start to the preparations for the European final.

Liverpool lay two points ahead in third place and they were next week's visitors. A top-three finish was a realistic possibility.

With another expensive day for supporters to come – the European final in Stockholm – the smallest League gate of the season had turned out. But in these blue days, it was bigger than the average gate for the previous season.

> *It wasn't the best of our performances but I think that's quite understandable because of what happened three days ago. We kept a clean sheet so we defended well. Football is all about pressing and pushing forward, sometimes to play nice football is difficult. That's why sometimes we play a long ball and try to win the second ball. We played a long ball from our half, Sparky flicked the ball for Tore and we've got a penalty – not playing nice football.*
>
> Gianluca Vialli

	Chelsea	Sheff Wed
Shots on target	4	2
Woodwork	1	2
Corners	3	3
Fouls	17	20
Offsides	3	8
Bookings	1	2

M Hughes, foul (66); Carbone on Granville (28), Di Canio on Lebeouf (31).

	Chelsea	Sheff Wed
Goals	1	0
Leboeuf (pen) (22)		
Assist		
Flo		

Saturday 25 April
Stamford Bridge
34,639

Chelsea 4 Liverpool 1

TOP-FIVE TEAM BEATEN IN LEAGUE FOR FIRST TIME IN OVER A YEAR

Vialli had no problems with his focus. He wrote: 'We are three weeks away from the end of the season. We've had a great season so far. It's up to us to make it an extraordinary one – or not! Everybody knows what we have to do if we are to make it extraordinary, It doesn't mean that I don't care about the Premier League. It means that we are going to use our spare matches in the League to keep the team fit and to improve on our weaknesses and of course to make everyone ready for the Final.'

On that score there was some success and some failure. The failure came after twenty-eight minutes. Zola, feeling more confident than at any time in the season, raced away from

time a quarter of an hour later he had already changed and gone home. He had two-and-a-half weeks to recover for the European Final, and tears take anything from four to six weeks to mend. Like Wise, he seemed to have no chance.

He flew to Italy where he was to receive non-stop treatment from the man who had looked after him at Parma. He wasn't seen again at Chelsea until the Friday before the Final.

At the time of the injury Chelsea were 1–0 up and in total charge. In the first two minutes Friedel had saved Hughes' header and Le Saux's shot and seen Zola's effort from the edge of the area deflect off a defender onto the bar.

Mark Hughes copyright: 'Sparky' scissor-kicks Chelsea's fourth goal

Liverpool's defence onto Petrescu's pass, but before he could attack Friedel he felt an agonizing tear in his groin. Desperately he tried a lob but the ball flopped to the goalkeeper.

He turned and limped away behind the goal and, helped by Mike Banks, down the tunnel. He was in acute pain.

When the players and staff reached the dressing room for half-

Hughes had headed Chelsea into the lead on ten minutes. A good period of keep-ball finished with what looked an unnecessarily early cross by Clarke, but Hughes outjumped Matteo and lobbed in.

Flo came on for Zola and typically picked up the pace of the game immediately. He was still looking so much sharper as a

Chelsea

Kharine

Clarke   Leboeuf   Myers   Le Saux

Petrescu   Newton   Di Matteo   Poyet
(Charvet 76)

M Hughes   Zola
(Nicholls 81) (Flo 30)

*Referee: **Gerald Ashby** (Worcester)*

Riedle   Murphy
(Thompson 76) (Berger 71)

Leonhardsen   Ince   Carragher   McManaman
(McAteer 76)

Bjornebye   Babb   Matteo   Jones

Friedel

Liverpool

substitute than when starting. But it shouldn't be forgotten that his season had started over a year previously, in March, in Norway, and he had enjoyed no break since.

Chelsea dominated right up to half-time. Hughes flashed a shot across the six-yard box when a pull back to Flo would have been better, Friedel smothered well from Poyet's header after Clarke and Flo had combined well, and he superbly tipped round Leboeuf's extravagant twenty-five-yard free-kick.

But right on the whistle Leboeuf was beaten by Murphy whose low eighteen-yard cross shot was palmed out by Kharine only for Riedle to tuck it in. What a waste of forty-five good minutes!

Liverpool gained confidence from that and looked the better team early in the second-half. Kharine blocked well from Riedle after McManaman had got his first penetrating run going, and then the German took advantage of slack defending to have a shot deflected wide.

But Chelsea were confident enough to battle back, and Friedel had to turn away another twenty-five-yarder, this time from Poyet. It was entertaining fare.

After sixty-seven minutes Chelsea took the lead with one of the most warmly greeted goals of the season. Steve Clarke, in his 417th Chelsea match, scored his first goal for six years, his first since his 196th game, and his tenth in all. He was up for a corner which was cleared, Leboeuf cleverly knocked the ball back in, Flo held off Babb to let it run on and Clarke held off McManaman before turning and planting an unstoppable ten-yard left-footer in the net.

He turned and ran backwards to the Matthew Harding Stand so he could see all his colleagues sprinting towards him. What a marvellous way to

move to the end of the season. Clarkey on the scoresheet! The whole ground sang his name. It was end-of-season party time.

Chelsea quickly turned the screw with their superior football. Flo raced away onto Le Saux's pass after Petrescu had nicked the ball, drew Friedel and slammed number three past him. It was his fifteenth goal of the season, and in a few more minutes Hughes collected his thirteenth.

If his strike against Vicenza had been a trademark dramatic matchwinning volley, this was a trademark scissors kick. 'We'd been trying to get a flick-on at the near post all afternoon and eventually we got it right,' he said. Duberry flicked on Di Matteo's wide free-kick. 'It was a little bit high I thought initially, but I was able to stretch a little bit and I got a good connection and in it went.' The ball shot off his athletic overhead strike and past the startled Friedel. 'I was telling them, law of averages, if I keep trying hard enough one will eventually go in. So there's my one for the season.'

The game finished pulsatingly with Kharine making a remarkable double save from Berger and Ince and Di Matteo just not reaching Flo's cross to make it five.

Chelsea rose to third with three games to go. They had sixty points, equal to the highest total they had collected in the top flight for twelve years, whether from thirty-eight games or forty-two! A top-three finish and a European victory would arguably make this the greatest Chelsea season of all time.

But of course Zola had joined Wise on the injury list. The advantage Chelsea had when winning the semi-final – knowing that Stuttgart defenders Verlaat and Spanring would be suspended for the final – was slipping away.

	Chelsea	Liverpool
Shots on target	13	5
Woodwork	1	0
Corners	8	4
Fouls	10	13
Offsides	3	6
Bookings	1	1

Leboeuf, foul (52); Ince on Poyet (59).

> *Liverpool is a great side. Stuttgart is a great side too. If we play like we played this afternoon I am confident we can get something out of the final.*
>
> **Gianluca Vialli**

	Chelsea	Liverpool
Goals	4	1

M Hughes (10, 77), Clarke (67), Flo (71); Riedle (45)

Assists

Clarke, Flo, Le Saux

Wednesday 29 April
Stamford Bridge
33,311

Chelsea 0 Blackburn Rovers 1

THIRD PLACE THROWN AWAY AGAINST BOGEY SIDE

So much for the top-five problem being defeated. Blackburn were in a dreadful run, two wins in fourteen games, and having led the challenge to Manchester United for much of the season were now staring failure to qualify for the UEFA Cup in the face.

Maybe Blackburn were like Leeds, strong, robust, aggressive. Maybe that's why they were Chelsea's jinx team. Chelsea hadn't beaten them in the League since 1984. Blackburn! An unbelievable sequence.

I missed this game. It was the first Chelsea game I'd missed in many years, but I was hospitalized and joined Wise and Zola in the race to be fit for Stockholm.

Vialli was using substitutions in order to keep everyone fresh for Stockholm, and he used up all three with twenty minutes to go. Unfortunately Le Saux then suffered a kick on the calf, and he became the third big name in four games to join the race for the Final.

As his departure would have meant Chelsea going down to ten men he stayed on the pitch to the end, but as soon as he came off his calf stiffened up badly.

Stuck in my hospital bed with no television or telephone, I had to make do with Radio Five Live which was concentrating on Arsenal professionally one-nilling Derby and moving to within one game of the title. Chelsea received just the occasional mention.

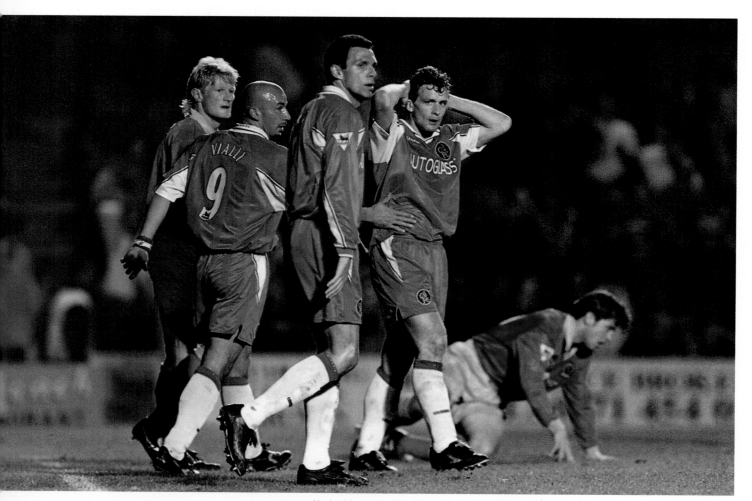

Hughes' frustration: the striker sees his shot hit the post

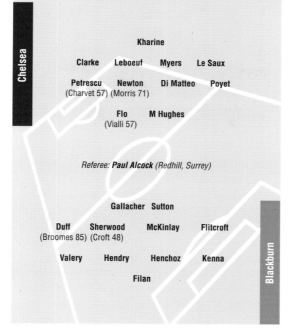

Chelsea

Kharine

Clarke   Leboeuf   Myers   Le Saux

Petrescu   Newton   Di Matteo   Poyet
(Charvet 57) (Morris 71)

Flo   M Hughes
(Vialli 57)

*Referee: **Paul Alcock** (Redhill, Surrey)*

Gallacher   Sutton

Duff   Sherwood   McKinlay   Flitcroft
(Broomes 85) (Croft 48)

Valery   Hendry   Henchoz   Kenna

Filan

Blackburn

Arsenal were behind Chelsea for so much of the season and even though everyone was raving about their two French midfielders, Vieira and Petit, you wouldn't consider either of them for the France national team ahead of Juventus' Zidane and Deschamps. They weren't in the same class.

Defensively they were magnificent. But on the ball they were erratic. Chelsea had so much more to offer.

Bergkamp won the individual awards – Player of the Year and Footballer of the Year – but they never missed him when he didn't play. The individual they kept missing, and whose return to fitness and form turned their season round, was defender Tony Adams.

Had Chelsea's failure to challenge throughout the season for the Premiership been caused by the defence? That's what the media said. But surprisingly Chelsea's problems had come in the period when the goalscoring dried up.

They had been unable then to claim a few 0–0 draws, or keep games at 0–0 until a decisive chance might finally unveil itself. In an extraordinary campaign, Chelsea drew just three out of thirty-eight Premiership games, by an enormous margin the fewest draws in the division.

But it wasn't that simple either. This was Chelsea's fifty-second game of the season in all competitions, and there had been sixteen clean sheets. That was one of the best returns in the League. It's just that early in the season when one was conceded more always followed, and in the middle of the season when none were scored one was always conceded.

Graham Rix wasn't apologizing for any of this. 'We're not a defensive team.

Everyone knows it. We're not the sort of side who's going to win 1–0 three games on the trot. You want clean sheets. But I want our players to have freedom when they've got the ball.' And he noted that Blackburn had lost their way despite having an outstanding defensive record for much of the season. 'I think maybe the fact that they weren't scoring goals as freely as we were, they altered their attitude a little bit and maybe a few gaps opened at the back. Always there are advantages and disadvantages to everything you do.'

Duberry had also joined the injured list now. Newton was still struggling when asked to play two games in a week and he was substituted along with Petrescu who must have been concerned with the number of times he had been hauled off.

Myers' dreadful mistake gave Gallacher a clear run on goal after two minutes but Kharine pulled off a wonderful diving save. The Russian went on to have his best game since returning to fitness.

Petrescu had a header saved, but early in the second-half Leboeuf inexplicably sliced over Duff's low cross and Gallacher finished off the simple chance.

In the last few minutes Hughes hammered Le Saux's cross against the outside of the post when he should have scored, Leboeuf blasted a twenty-yard free-kick against the angle of post and bar, and the Frenchman also had a dramatic shout for a penalty in stoppage time.

So, in front of a healthily large crowd, it wasn't all bad. But the defeat gave Liverpool the chance to leapfrog back into third place.

> '*They scored and we lost our shape. With thirty-five, forty minutes to go we didn't need to be so aggressive and play taking so many risks. There was still time to recover playing our football. We must put this right before the Final.*'
> **Gianluca Vialli**

	Chelsea	Blackburn
Shots on target	3	3
Woodwork	2	0
Corners	9	2
Fouls	13	18
Offsides	1	3
Bookings	0	0

	Chelsea	Blackburn
Goals	0	1
Gallacher (47)		

Saturday 2 May
St James' Park
36,710

Newcastle United 3 Chelsea 1

FIFTEENTH LEAGUE DEFEAT OF THE SEASON

I was missing again, out of hospital but not strong enough to travel. Chelsea were missing too. Newcastle were still in relegation trouble, but Chelsea did nothing to avoid defeat. Zola was still in Italy and contrary to media reports of agony on the beach was beginning to run and building optimism. Wise had returned to Italy for a second period of treatment.

But back home Le Saux's calf sprain was worse than at first feared and he was becoming a major European Final doubt. Danny Granville took his place for this game, his twenty-fourth time in Chelsea colours. He had acquitted himself well and, bar one or two lapses of concentration, had been reliable. He had scored that important second goal at home to Slovan Bratislava in the first

round of the Cup Winners' Cup. He hadn't set the place alight, but you could do worse than rely on him.

The left-hand side had been a real problem for Chelsea. When they were flourishing at the beginning of the season with Le Saux and Poyet it looked magnificent. Poyet's injury was a major blow, and both Babayaro and Le Saux looked more comfortable at left-back than in midfield.

Both of them, however, suffered injuries, Babayaro's turning out to be the most serious. In and out of plaster all season as his stress-fractured foot refused to mend, the strong, fast and hugely talented player turned into Chelsea's biggest loss of the campaign.

Both Nicholls and Granville did their bit on the left to keep the

Kharine punches clear from Newton and Andersson

Newcastle

Given

Dabizas Howey Pearce
(Watson 46)

Barton Lee Batty Speed Pistone
(Hamilton 84)

Shearer Andersson
(Barnes 80)

*Referee: **Keith Burge** (Tonypandy)*

Vialli M Hughes
(Flo 46)

Morris Di Matteo Newton Nicholls
(P Hughes 78)

Granville Leboeuf Charvet Clarke
(Poyet 46)

Kharine

Chelsea

season going, but even though Le Saux may not have had the most outstanding of campaigns, it was always noticeable when he wasn't there. You realized just how fast and effective he was. So did his fellow professionals who voted him into the PFA Divisional team, the only Chelsea player to achieve the honour this season.

If Granville was to do more than just a job, it was time for him to step up a gear.

Duberry was missing again, this time with the most severe bout of tonsillitis Mike Banks had ever seen. Chelsea put Charvet at centre-half. Charvet had come to Chelsea as a wing-back or right-winger. He was strong in the air, very fast, and well built. But he had no special defensive talents. On the day, however, he did well enough. This was especially impressive as he had already been told he would not be retained at the end of the season. Chelsea would have to pay £800,000 to make the loan permanent, and that was thought too much.

On the day Chelsea never looked like holding on to 0–0 or breaking Newcastle down. The midfield was overrun. Morris was out of sorts and Newton was still struggling. A lot of people needed rest and a full pre-season.

Defeat here was Chelsea's fifteenth in the League all season. Liverpool beat West Ham to leapfrog Chelsea. The three teams above the Blues finished with six, seven and nine defeats. Only Derby in the top half of the Premiership finished with as many defeats.

On the last day of the season, the following week, when Bolton travelled to Stamford Bridge to try and avoid defeat and relegation, they had lost exactly the same number of games as Chelsea – fifteen. The difference was they had won nine and drawn thirteen while Chelsea had won

nineteen and drawn three, and were about to win a twentieth.

The details at St James' Park were horrible. Vialli and Pearce got in a bust-up and were booked. Vialli fouled Dabizas near the halfway line and was lucky not to be sent off for a second yellow card offence. Lee's long free-kick was attacked by Dabizas while Hughes stopped and watched, and the Greek sent a free header home for his first Premiership goal.

Three minutes later Shearer chased an overhit cross, shimmied wide of Granville and crossed back for Lee to dart ahead of Clarke and head in. In between the two goals Kharine had crucially punched clear from Lee. Leboeuf brought down Andersson, was booked, and was not risked for the second-half. He was replaced by Poyet so Chelsea now had two midfielders in central defence.

Newcastle wrapped it up just before the hour when Speed ghosted in behind Morris to take Pistone's pass and drive it through Charvet and beyond Kharine.

Chelsea were better in the last fifteen minutes, and Granville's surging run to the penalty area set up Di Matteo to turn away from Dabizas and inside Lee before striking his tenth goal of the season from just inside the area.

Twenty-seven years ago an outstanding Chelsea side had won the European Cup Winners' Cup. It was a side regularly drunk on glory but never solid enough to win the Championship. Twenty-seven years on a team which was beginning to look even better still needed the extra steel required to pull off the big one.

But it didn't matter. The big one for this season was still to come, and victory would turn it into a glorious year to match any other in the club's history.

> **The team will finish higher than last season, that shows how we are improving. Everything about the club is getting better, the stadium, the facilities. We all want to move towards first place in the Premiership.**
>
> Gianluca Vialli

	Newcastle	Chelsea
Shots on target	9	2
Corners	8	3
Fouls	18	22
Offsides	4	2
Bookings	1	2

Pearce, flare-up with Vialli (26); Vialli, flare-up (26), Leboeuf, foul (45).

	Newcastle	Chelsea
Goals	3	1

Dabizas (39), Lee (42), Speed (59); Di Matteo (78)

Sunday 10 May
Stamford Bridge
34,845

Chelsea 2 Bolton Wanderers 0

FIFTH-BEST LEAGUE FINISH IN CHELSEA'S HISTORY

Chelsea could not finish third. A midweek win by Liverpool had put that beyond them. Victory would give them a finish of fourth, the fifth-best finish in their ninety-three-year history. Defeat allied to Leeds beating Wimbledon would mean a finish of fifth. They could drop no lower than that.

The nation was focused on this game and Everton's home match against Coventry. Crystal Palace and Barnsley were already relegated, but either Everton or Bolton would join them. Everton were a point behind Bolton.

Chelsea had asked for the games to be brought forward to Saturday so they could prepare properly for the European Cup Winners' Cup Final, but the Premier League had refused the request. Gianluca Vialli wasn't overly concerned, even though Wednesday's opponents Stuttgart had no such pressures. He was aware

that a proper team was put out despite the European final so that the relegation issue didn't become a farce.

More important than anything else to Chelsea, however, was the players' fitness for the European Cup Winners' Cup Final. Vialli had said he would like everyone who was going to declare themselves fit for Wednesday to take some part in today's game. But that wasn't going to be possible.

Wise, miraculously, had started full training – very gingerly – on Friday. He agreed to play one half. Duberry had also started on Friday following his tonsillitis, but had now developed palsy, a frozen face with no feeling down one side. He didn't play. Zola's return to full training had been put off to the following day. Le Saux was increasingly doubtful. Sinclair was definitely out as his groin strain had been followed by a calf strain.

Jody Morris scores the last League goal of the season

aware that a week earlier Inter Milan had played Vicenza on Sunday and then thrashed Lazio 3-0 in the UEFA Cup Final on Wednesday.

Many Chelsea supporters made no pretence of the fact they would rather Bolton survive in the Premiership than wealthy Everton. Media attention focused on Chelsea all week, concerned

Chelsea continued with the experiment of playing Charvet at the back, and although he and Leboeuf lacked strength they got Chelsea playing lovely football from base and provided the speediest, most mobile back line you could wish to see. De Goey returned in goal to prepare for Wednesday.

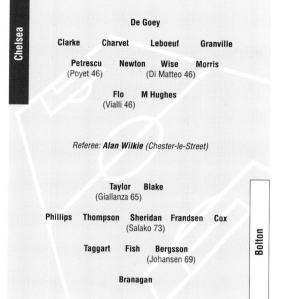

Chelsea

De Goey

Clarke   Charvet   Leboeuf   Granville

Petrescu   Newton   Wise   Morris
(Poyet 46)   (Di Matteo 46)

Flo   M Hughes
(Vialli 46)

*Referee: **Alan Wilkie** (Chester-le-Street)*

Taylor   Blake
(Giallanza 65)

Phillips   Thompson   Sheridan   Frandsen   Cox
(Salako 73)

Taggart   Fish   Bergsson
(Johansen 69)

Branagan

Bolton

Chelsea managed to cram in the biggest Stamford Bridge crowd of the season. Wise started brightly, beating two challenges to find Di Matteo. The ball was worked out to Newton whose fine pass fed Petrescu and his shot was deflected for a corner.

Bolton had the best of the next thirty minutes as Chelsea cruised in third gear. Chelsea weren't negative, but they weren't wild either. Bolton had chances and de Goey blocked well from Sheridan and was relieved to see Leboeuf deflect Thompson's header over.

But the best save was Wise's after Frandsen fastened onto a Bolton clearance, sprinted past Leboeuf, turned inside Charvet on the edge of the area and beat de Goey with his shot. Wise sprinted back from nowhere to turn the ball away from the goalmouth.

The remarkable thing about his save was that it required his left foot, and it was virtually the first time he had kicked the ball with his left foot all afternoon. If he had to play himself into the final by turning out today and giving a one-legged performance, that was what he was going to do. Before half-time he even forced Branagan into his first save.

Vialli used all his three substitutes at half-time, and they were all effective. Most effective of all was Vialli himself. Bolton, to be honest, were not a good team, and did not have the technical quality to cope with a third-gear Chelsea. It was an honest performance but it wasn't a Premiership one.

Their fans, however, were magnificent,

cheering their side on. Everton were winning at half-time. Bolton, therefore, needed a win. So they changed from 3–5–2 to 4–4–2, but within three minutes South African defender Fish was caught upfield, Vialli appeared in the gap and Morris fed him perfectly. Vialli stabbed the ball past the advancing Branagan and Bolton's dreams appeared over.

With five minutes left Everton conceded an equalizer. A Bolton draw would do. Their crowd went crazy. Chelsea's crowd joined them. 'Let them score, let them score, let them score…'

Bolton nearly did, but Thompson had no right foot to shoot and his dink into the area was missed by Giallanza. Almost immediately Thompson lost the ball to Newton's athletic tackle, and Poyet raced away to find Morris running alone, and the youngster almost apologetically put the ball in the net. One minute to go. Goodnight Bolton.

Their sporting fans sang 'One Team In Europe' in response to Chelsea's sympathetic applause, and next day the Bolton FC switchboard was inundated with calls of sympathy and good wishes from Chelsea fans. Good luck next year, Wanderers!

Meanwhile, the annual lap of appreciation had some honourable silverware. The Coca-Cola Cup was brought out. Chelsea were fourth in the League and one of the finest sides in the club's history. They were also one match away from becoming, arguably, the finest.

What an amazing year!

> ❛ *We have to be pleased. We finished fourth and also we got the Coca-Cola Cup and also are in the final of Cup Winners' Cup, so it is a great season so far, and if we succeed in the Cup Winners' Cup then we can say it is an extraordinary season.* ❜
>
> **Gianfranco Zola**

> ❛ *Fourth is a good place. Chelsea in the last years has never been that high. We started this two years ago when a few players came over, and we hope to stay here and we hope to carry on and get better and better.* ❜
>
> **Roberto Di Matteo**

	Chelsea	Bolton
Shots on target	5	7
Corners	4	12
Fouls	14	9
Offsides	6	8
Bookings	2	1

Charvet, foul (18), Leboeuf, foul (58); Cox on Leboeuf (64).

	Chelsea	Bolton
Goals	2	0

Vialli (72), Morris (89)

Assists

Morris, Poyet

Wednesday 13 May
Råsunda Stadium, Stockholm
30,216

Chelsea 1 VfB Stuttgart 0

IT'S A BLUE YEAR AS CHELSEA WIN CUP DOUBLE

Gianfranco Zola didn't make the starting line-up. He had to make do with coming on as a substitute after seventy minutes. Seventeen seconds later he won the European Cup Winners' Cup with a glorious half-volley from Dennis Wise's pass. The two crocks who miraculously beat the fitness deadline had established themselves as central to a great, great Chelsea team.

Zola had started full training at Harlington on the Monday and come through with no problems. Duberry was in full training but Le Saux was a definite non-starter.

The whole squad, including the injured Le Saux, Sinclair and Babayaro, travelled to Stockholm on the Tuesday. The huge airlift and coach shuttle of Chelsea fans started then too. Figures vary on how many supporters made the trip, but it must have been about 15,000. Stuttgart took just under 4,000.

All but the injured three trained on Tuesday evening in the stadium and again on Wednesday morning. But at that final training session Vialli took Zola to one side and told him he couldn't risk him for ninety minutes. 'I was fit and I felt that I could play easily,' Zola claimed later. 'It was a little bit disappointing not to start from the beginning. When I recovered from my injury I thought the work was done. I expected to play. But it's okay. I turned all the frustration into positive things.'

Wise fires fractionally wide at 0–0

Zola scores the spectacular winner

Flo got the vote to partner Vialli – the opposite partnership to the Coca-Cola Final – with Vialli saying Flo was a fifteen-million-pound player. Duberry was still suffering dreadfully with palsy but was selected. Given his state of health, his heroics were never properly recognized.

At left-back Granville took his leap into the biggest of big times wonderfully. Defensively he was a giant. Going forward he was increasingly influential. By the end of the evening he could say he had been a star in a European final. What a bargain buy he had turned out to be.

On the opposite flank Steve Clarke played his 421st Chelsea game. That took him past Kerry Dixon into fourth place in Chelsea's all time appearances list. 'It was a good game to do it in,' smiled the exhausted thirty-four-year-old Scotsman in the dressing room afterwards. 'It's quite an emotional night. I'm not getting any younger, and there's every chance that's the last time I'll play in a game like that, so it's a hell of an occasion for me. It's been a good year. Three winners' medals in twelve months after a long time not winning anything. You can imagine what it means to me.'

For the one-off final Vialli returned to the midfield diamond that started the season. Lined up against them were a powerful Stuttgart side who had finished fourth in the high-quality Bundesliga. Thus both sides had already qualified for next season's UEFA Cup.

The pitch was a disgrace. It was uneven, patchy, and not worthy of any kind of final. But Chelsea mastered it better than Stuttgart.

The Blues started strongest, and after five minutes Di Matteo, Petrescu and Poyet combined with perfect Chelsea one-touch. Poyet's final square ball gave Di Matteo a left-foot shot from seventeen yards but he hooked it just wide.

Then Stuttgart had the better of the combat for ten minutes. Nothing dramatic, but Chelsea needed to defend stoutly.

Granville headed away a poor Haber cross after Akpoborie had taken advantage of Duberry losing possession; Bobic raced away from Clarke's miscue but blazed pathetically over; Duberry got in two crucial tackles in a row in the box, the second going for a corner from which Schneider's far-post header scudded just wide; and after eighteen minutes Stuttgart had the first shot on target.

Bobic, who was spending too much time diving and acting injured, showed his real class with a great break from midfield. Balakov latched onto his pass, took the ball in the box but de Goey responded brilliantly to palm away his left-foot shot. Duberry cleaned up the loose ball with another aggressive interception.

Balakov was meant to be Stuttgart's main creator, but that was all we really saw from him. Wise got tighter on him and started running the show.

Later, media reports suggested Stuttgart had the better of the first-half. That was rubbish. They had ten minutes, they had the first frightening shot, but you would expect them to carry some threat against any side in the world, given their status.

After the game Leboeuf and Duberry were forceful in their response to people who said Chelsea couldn't defend well enough. 'Three Cup Finals, three clean sheets!' the Frenchman pointed out.

Chelsea quickly came back with Flo hooking Leboeuf's free-kick over a defender and then heading it over the advancing Wohlfahrt onto the roof of the net. This was the same goalkeeper whom John Spencer had beaten against Austria Memphis in his famous seventy-yard dash in 1994. But Wohlfahrt was to hold out a while longer now.

Duberry lost possession in his own half again and Wise took no chances, bringing down Balakov and suffering a yellow card which meant a one-match European suspension. He had kept himself in check all through the competition when it mattered, and his part in the team's victory underlined more than ever the fact that he should have been involved in England's World Cup journey.

On the half hour mark Gustavo Poyet struck Chelsea's first on-target effort, whipping a volley from Berthold's headed clearance so perfectly that Wohlfahrt could only throw his arms up and let the ball bounce off them. Just before half-time Wise volleyed fractionally wide when a free-kick was cleared to him. Chelsea went into the interval confident.

The celebrations begin ...

... and continue in the dressing room with champagne for Leboeuf

Five minutes into the second-half Balakov's back-flick to Soldo was met with a cross-shot that flashed just past Bobic and the far post. Thereafter Chelsea ruled.

Flo went round Schneider and crossed, and the ball was eventually worked by Vialli and Petrescu to Wise whose twenty-yarder was fractionally wide. Vialli had a shot easily held. Wise had another shot blocked after good work by Granville, and Chelsea worked the ball back to the left-back who this time shot low but Wohlfahrt held on at his right-hand post.

At the other end Granville was brilliant when de Goey's miskick gave the speedy Akpoborie a run at goal. Granville sprinted back past him to cover. That put the tension stakes up.

Chelsea's forwards had worked hard and shown threat, but hadn't finished off the job. Flo was tiring. Rix sent on Zola with twenty minutes remaining.

His first touch resulted in Yakin tackling him, the ball rebounded to Wise and Zola saw the gap quickly and darted forward between substitute Endress and Berthold. Wise's first-time lobbed half-volley was perfect. Zola's first-time crashed half-volley into the goal was phenomenal. Wohlfahrt was comprehensively beaten. Zola ran pointing to the Chelsea fans. What fans! What a player! What a team!

Stuttgart threw on attacking wingers in place of their wing-backs and won some corners but never really threatened. Chelsea's defence remained disciplined and confident. Poyet, tiring, tore a groin muscle but still stretched to get in a crucial tackle before making way for Newton. Newton went central and Di Matteo wide. Chelsea would play out time with a solid 4–4–2.

de Goey

Clarke   Duberry   Leboeuf   Granville

Wise

Petrescu   Poyet
                 (Newton 80)

Di Matteo

Vialli   Flo
         (Zola 70)

Referee: **Stefano Braschi** (Italy)

Bobic   Akpoborie

Balakov

Hagner   Poschner   Soldo   Haber
(Ristic 77)   (Djordjevic 74)

Berthold   Yakin   Schneider
                  (Endress 53)

Wohlfahrt

Or that was the plan. Four minutes later Petrescu was ludicrously sent off for a challenge on Yakin. Referee Braschi said his foot was raised when it wasn't. Chelsea were down to ten men.

Time was used up well, and when Wohlfahrt was caught forward in Chelsea's half and Stuttgart lost the ball on the edge of Chelsea's area, Granville raced forward with an open goal beckoning. Should he make for the corner or have a shot? In the end he crossed just ahead of Vialli and Chelsea won a corner. The otherwise impressive Poschner argued with Braschi as he raced back to defend and was yellow carded. He continued to argue and was sent off. Ten men each.

Chelsea kept the ball in the corner again and were in complete control when the final whistle went.

When Wise went up to lift the European Cup Winners' Cup he became the most successful Chelsea captain of all time. The Blues celebrated in all four corners of the ground. They danced and sang and ran the length of the pitch hand in hand and dived to the ground and did it all again and again and again.

Chelsea had won, Chelsea had deserved to win, Chelsea had two cups.

	Chelsea	Stuttgart
Shots on target	4	1
Corners	5	5
Fouls	17	23
Offsides	2	5
Bookings	1	1

Wise, foul (25); Akpoborie on Leboeuf (32).

Sendings off	1	1

Petrescu, foul (84); Poschner, two bookings for dissent (90).

> **We'll have a nice team photo at the start of next season 'cause we'll have a couple of trophies.**
>
> Dennis Wise

> **It wasn't a game I think in Stockholm, it just looked like a game at Stamford Bridge. The fans were magnificent.**
>
> Ed de Goey

> **I thought this is the moment, Franco, take it, and fortunately everything went right because I hit the ball perfectly and it went where I wanted it to go. It was absolutely magnificent.**
>
> Gianfranco Zola

The 15,000 fans danced out of the stadium while the team drank champagne in the dressing room. It had been the most wonderful year imaginable. Football doesn't get better than this.

Happy Gus grasps the Cup

	Chelsea	Stuttgart
Goal	1	0

Zola (70)

Assist

Wise

The Team

1 Ed de Goey
Goalkeeper

In his first season at Chelsea the tallest man ever to turn out for the Blues commendably overcame a dodgy start to perform outstandingly in the last six months and keep clean sheets in both Cup Finals. A £2.25m signing from Feyenoord, he was Holland's reserve goalkeeper. Games: 42. Clean sheets: 16.

2 Dan Petrescu
Midfield

Converted from right wing-back in the sweeper system to an attacking right-sided midfielder, the man with the perfect first touch scored his share of goals and was second in the assists list to Zola. Vice-captain of Romania, as the season wore on he found himself substituted too often, including in the Coca-Cola Cup Final. Harshly sent off in the European Cup Winners' Cup Final. Games: 42 (+1 sub). Goals: 8.

3 Celestine Babayaro
Defender

Chelsea's record teenage buy, £2.25m from Anderlecht in the summer, he was desperately unlucky with injuries. A problematic groin strain was followed by two stress fractures of the foot. When he played he showed strength, determination and good positioning. He has pace and skill and will surely be a star of the future. Games: 11(+2 sub).

4 Ruud Gullit
Defender, midfielder, striker

Once the best player in the world, not so long ago surely the best player ever to wear Chelsea blue but the strains of management limited his fitness and consequently his performances. Controversially dismissed as manager in February over ridiculous wage demands, when the acrimony has died down he will be remembered as one of the best managers of the club even though he was in charge for just twenty-one months. Games: 3 (+7 sub).

5 Frank Leboeuf
Defender

Adjusted from sweeper to back four centre-half, the France reserve continued to use the ball with far superior ability to any other defender in the country. Chelsea's highest appearance maker in a wonderful season, and still their 100 percent successful penalty taker. Games: 47. Goals: 6.

6 Steve Clarke
Defender

The wily veteran and vice-captain probably played more games than he expected, but because his defensive knowledge was so vast that was no problem. A substitute in the second-half of the Coca-Cola Final and a starter in the European final in a game which made him Chelsea's all-time fourth top appearance maker. He even scored his first goal in six years. Games: 34 (+7 sub). Goals: 1.

7 Bernard Lambourde
Defender, midfielder

Summer £1.5m signing from Bordeaux, he found it difficult to adjust after injury to the physical nature and pace of the English game and settled better in midfield than in his natural defensive role. Games: 9 (+4 sub).

8 Gustavo Poyet
Midfielder

An instant hit, the summer free signing from Real Zaragoza brought class, height and goals to the left of Chelsea's midfield and was fundamental to the wonderful start to the season. The Uruguayan international overcame a cruciate ligament rupture to return within six months and reclaim his place with a European semi-final goal and Final appearance. Games: 16 (+3 sub). Goals: 5.

9 Gianluca Vialli
Forward

Four goals at Barnsley, two in the snow at Tromsø and a hat-trick in the return marked this out as a special second season for the man who wanted to be a Chelsea legend. In February he replaced Gullit as player-manager and managed the Blues to two Cup wins, playing in the European one where he won his fourth European winners' medal. Top scorer. A legend indeed. Games: 24 (+10 sub). Goals: 19.

10 Mark Hughes
Forward

He may have been thirty-four in November, but Chelsea's reigning Player of the Year had another season to remember with a good goals return. He scored in both legs of the Coca-Cola Cup semi-final and blazed the winner in the European Cup Winners' Cup semi-final. Played the first Final and was an unused substitute in the second. Games: 30 (+10 sub). Goals: 13.

11 Dennis Wise
Midfielder

The most successful captain in Chelsea's history having lifted three major trophies. His move to the anchor of midfield led to a truly outstanding season despite the fact that he rarely trained because of injury. Suspended too often, but look at the three Cup Final goals: his passes made two of them and released Flo to win the corner for the third. He passed the 300 game milestone midway through the season. A great Chelsea player at his peak. Deservedly, he was Player of the Year. Games: 40. Goals: 3.

12 Michael Duberry
Defender

Missed pre-season while he recovered from a ruptured Achilles tendon, he was rushed back to first team duty because of his defensive presence. He then had to adjust first to a back four and then to a more direct style of game. It wasn't always easy, but he remained an unarguable first choice and was excellent in both Cup Finals, especially the European one where he overcame illness to play. Games: 33.

13 Kevin Hitchcock
Goalkeeper

The substitute goalkeeper whoever is fit and available because of his unique attitude and preparation towards the team winning. Such quality of approach won him a new one-year contract at the end of his benefit season. Games: 2.

14 Graeme Le Saux
Defender

Chelsea's record purchase at £5m as the season began, Le Saux returned to where his career started. A spell in midfield proved he is still adaptable, but at left-back he is clearly one of the first in the game. Injury forced him to miss the European Final, but the Coca-Cola Cup victory was his first Cup triumph. England's left wing-back was also selected as the PFA Divisional left-back. Games: 34. Goals: 3.

15 David Lee
Defender

Found it hard to regain match fitness following a year out with a broken leg, he improved after a month's loan at Sheffield United but was not registered for the second half of the European campaign. Games: 1 (+2 sub).

16 Roberto Di Matteo
Midfielder

In his second season he followed up his famous FA Cup Final goal with a thirty-yard Coca-Cola Cup semi-final scorcher and a Final strike too. Italy regular, his attacking runs from midfield remained a constant problem for Premiership and European opposition. Remarkably, he didn't score in the European Final. Games: 42 (+2 sub). Goals: 10.

17 Danny Granville
Defender

In his first full season following a transfer from Cambridge United, he played all pre-season and in the Charity Shield but then lost out to Le Saux. Reliable cover when required, he returned for the last few games including the European Final where he gave a performance of the highest quality. Games: 16 (+5 sub). Goals: 1.

18 Andy Myers
Defender

Converted to central defence, at the age of twenty-four he passed the 100 games landmark for the Blues, and was involved in a high number of clean sheets. As fast and competitive as ever, but still too injury prone. Unused substitute in the European Final. Games: 12 (+4 sub).

19 Tore Andre Flo
Forward

Bargain £300,000 signing from Branne Bergen in his native Norway, he scored three minutes into his debut, hit a hat-trick at Tottenham, two goals at Real Betis, a bundle of goals when coming on as substitute and proved himself a top international star. Tall, fast and tricky. An effective substitute in the Coca-Cola Final and starter in the European Final. Games: 23 (+21 sub) Goals: 15

20 Frank Sinclair
Defender

Arguably Chelsea's most improved player, apart from a bumpy Christmas and New Year the right-back had an excellent season during which he passed 200 games for the club, gained international recognition from Jamaica and scored the opening Coca-Cola Cup Final goal. Injury, however, robbed him of a European Final place. Games: 30 (+3 sub). Goals: 3.

21 Paul Hughes
Defender, midfielder
Followed his first taste of first team duty the previous term by finding himself in defence for the first time in his life early in the season. He battled hard but is clearly a ball-playing midfielder. Games: 6 (+4 sub).

22 Mark Nicholls
Midfielder, forward
An outstanding first half of the season, mostly off the substitutes' bench, earned him several opportunities as an attacking midfielder, but the neat and confident youngster found appearances hard to come by as the season developed. Games: 11 (+13 sub). Goals: 3.

23 Dmitri Kharine
Goalkeeper
Returned to the first team in February after eighteen months out with the second ruptured cruciate ligament of his career. The former Russian international needed games to rebuild his outstanding ability and by the end of the season looked more like his old self. Games: 10. Clean sheets: 2.

24 Eddie Newton
Midfielder
A summer knee operation robbed him of his second successive pre-season, but injuries to others and his dogged reliability in midfield meant he was rushed back to first team duty again. He played his 200th Chelsea game, started the Coca-Cola Final and was a substitute in the European one. Not his best season, but his best return of medals! Games: 26 (+3 sub).

25 Gianfranco Zola
Forward
The superlative skills which earned Zola Chelsea's first-ever English Footballer of the Year award the previous season were not so consistently to the fore this campaign, but once again he topped the assists list by a mile. He scored the best hat-trick you could ever see against Derby, and after playing all two hours of the Coca-Cola Final beat injury to come off the bench and score the European Final winner with a dramatic shot. An absolute star. Games: 36 (+5 sub). Goals: 12.

26 Laurent Charvet
Midfielder, defender
Gullit's last signing, taken on loan from Cannes, the well-built and very fast right-sided player proved his adaptability by playing centre-back in the last two League games. Unused European Final substitute. Not retained at the end of the season. Games: 7 (+6 sub). Goals: 2.

28 Jody Morris
Midfield
A certain star of the future when he made his first team debut at seventeen and quickly established himself in England Under-21s two years previously, injury and a wavering attitude threatened his progress, especially in the first part of the season. But his return to the fold was climaxed with an excellent European semi-final second leg and a place on the bench for the Final. Games: 12 (+4 sub). Goals: 2.

32 Steven Hampshire
Forward, midfielder
Made his debut nine days after his eighteenth birthday while still a youth team player, but failed to win another chance. Games: 0 (+1 sub).

34 Nick Crittenden
Midfielder
Made an impressive debut in the Coca-Cola Cup and in his first year as a professional suggested potential. Games: 1 (+2 sub).

35 Jon Harley
Midfielder
An excellent debut at left wing-back in the victory at Derby, the eighteen-year-old FA School of Excellence graduate proved himself a neat ball player comfortable at first team level. Games: 3.

Graham Rix
Coach
Outstanding at the training ground and increasingly influential after the change of manager, the 'friend of the players' role' is one to which he is ideally suited.

Gwyn Williams
Assistant Manager
In these days of overseas players, aggressive youth policies and European opposition, the role Williams has developed after eighteen years at the club – father, godfather, assistant and nappy changer – is one that surely every top club will have to copy.

Eddie Niedzwiecki
Goalkeeping coach
The work required to help an overseas goalkeeper settle to Premiership football cannot be overestimated, and de Goey settled quickly after a very difficult start. Niedzwiecki was also an important scout.

Mike Banks
Physiotherapist
The days of the old spongeman have gone. A highly qualified leader of Chelsea's rehabilitation team.

Ade Mafe
Fitness And Conditioning Coach
Former Olympic 200 metres finalist responsible for getting the fit match fit and for returning those recovered from injury back to training fitness.

Terry Byrne
Assistant Physiotherapist
Head masseur, he also moves the injured players from the treatment-only stage to the physical activity stage and so spends more hours with them than anyone.

Mick McGiven
Reserve team coach
Oversees Chelsea's youth programme and scouts opposition.

Bob Orsborn
Kit Man
From towels to tissues via shirts and shorts.

Ken Bates
Chairman
As chairman of Chelsea Village he was more involved with the business – the development of Chelsea Village Hotel and the Chelsea Village facilities of restaurants, function rooms, bars and apartments plus. of course, the stadium's development – than the football side of things.

Colin Hutchinson
Managing Director
Responsible for the day-to-day running of the football club including negotiating transfers and new contracts. The man who replaced Gullit with Vialli.

Afterword

You're only as good as your next game. Chelsea celebrated their second trophy in six-and-a-half weeks by half the team splitting off to prepare for World Cup duty and the other half flying off for a two-match tournament and holiday break in Martinique.

With two trophies won as manager, Gianluca Vialli had rushed to the top of Chelsea's management tree. To take over from the superstar Ruud Gullit and finish a stuttering season successfully was a remarkable feat. But next he had to prove himself on the other side of management, he had to bring in the right players to strengthen the team for the next campaign.

'Chelsea can be thought of as one of the best teams in the world,' he said. 'This is a step forward towards a great future.' And that future, he left no doubt, was an assault upon the Premiership title, the English Championship which Chelsea have claimed just once.

Will it happen? Can Chelsea turn from big-match Cup glory specialists to consistent collectors of three points? Will there be a better opportunity than 1997/98, when Manchester United collapsed and Arsenal came from behind Chelsea, to win the title? Can Chelsea retain their place as the nation's top entertainers and the masters of cool?

The ground development is still to finish but the team's ability to excite just keeps on rolling. There is a clear path to progress along. It hasn't always been in Chelsea's genes to keep moving forward. But maybe, maybe this time.